25/11

THE LIFE OF
ST EDMUND
KING AND MARTYR

A FACSIMILE

THE LIFE OF ST EDMUND KING AND MARTYR

John Lydgate's Illustrated Verse Life Presented to Henry VI

A FACSIMILE OF
BRITISH LIBRARY MS HARLEY 2278

Introduction by
A. S. G. EDWARDS

THE BRITISH LIBRARY
2004

First published 2004 by The Folio Society
This edition published 2004 by
The British Library
96 Euston Road
London NW1 2DB

© in images 2004 The British Library Board
© in text 2004 A. S. G. Edwards

British Library Cataloguing in Publication Data
A CIP record for this book is available from The British Library

ISBN 0 7123 4871 9

Photography by Laurence Pordes
Facsimile production supervised by Joe Whitlock Blundell
Designed and typeset by Bob Elliott
Printed and bound in Great Britain by Cambridge Printing

PREFACE

British Library MS Harley 2278 is probably the most important illustrated manuscript of Middle English verse to be produced in the fifteenth century. The scale and quality of these illustrations are often mentioned in studies of the art of this period. But it has not hitherto been possible to demonstrate the extent of the manuscript's artistic achievement through a full facsimile.

I am much indebted to Professor James I. Miller for a copy of his Harvard thesis, an edition of Lydgate's poem. I owe long-standing debts to three friends who have shaped the study of English manuscripts of the second half of the fifteenth century: Ian Doyle, Derek Pearsall and Kathleen Scott. If it is proper to dedicate this facsimile it must be to them for the example and constant stimulus of their scholarship. I owe much to Julia Boffey that I do not wish to put into words.

A. S. G. Edwards

INTRODUCTION

On Christmas Eve, 1433, the young Henry VI arrived at the Benedictine Abbey at Bury St Edmunds. His intention was not just to celebrate Christmas there but to remain at the Abbey until after Easter, 1434, as a cost-saving measure for the royal household. The Abbey had little time to prepare for this visit, which required the completion within a month of extensive repairs to the abbot's palace and the organization of appropriate ceremonial to mark the arrival of the king and his large entourage.

Henry was received by 500 of the townspeople of Bury St Edmunds, in red livery, and met by his confessor, William Alnwick, Bishop of Norwich, and by the Abbot, William Curteys. The king's time there was divided between the Abbey itself and the abbot's palace at Elmswell. After Easter, on 23 April 1434, when he was about to depart, Henry was admitted to the Abbey's confraternity and marked his admission by prostrating himself before the shrine of the Abbey's patron, St Edmund.[1]

The choice of the Abbey at Bury St Edmunds for such an extended royal sojourn was not a surprising one. It was one of the largest and wealthiest religious foundations in fifteenth-century England.[2] It was presided over by William Curteys, Abbot from 1429 to 1446. It was a measure of Curteys's ability as well as the status of the Abbey that such a protracted visit was so successfully organized. In later years he was to prove a loyal servant to the king, who turned to him for help in raising money.[3] Near the end of his time as abbot, in 1446, he celebrated Mass at King's College, Cambridge on the occasion of its foundation by Henry.

It was natural for such an adroit clerical politician to seek to mark the king's long stay in the Abbey in some distinctive way. The strategy he chose for doing so is best expressed in the words of the one charged with implementing it, John Lydgate, a monk of the Abbey:

> In this mater there is no more to seyn,
> Sauf* to the kyng for to do plesaunce*,   *except *pleasure
> Thabbot William, his humble chapeleyn,

---

[1] Henry's visit to the Abbey and the preparations for it are recorded in Curteys's Register, now British Library Add. MS 14848, fol. 128r-v; this passage is reprinted in Craven Ord, 'Account of the Entertainment of King Henry the Sixth at the Abbey of Bury St Edmunds', *Archaeologia*, 15 (1806), 65–71.

[2] For a concise account of the Abbey see Walter F. Schirmer, *John Lydgate, A Study in the Culture of the XVth Century*, tr. Ann E. Keep (London: Methuen, 1961), pp. 8–23.

[3] On Curteys's career see the brief account in T. Arnold, ed., *Memorials of Bury St Edmund's Abbey*, 3 vols (Rolls Series, 189–96), III, xxix–xxxiii.

> Gaf me in charge to do myn attendaunce* *service
> The noble story to translate in substaunce* *in general
> Out of the latyn aftir my kunnyng* **according to my skill*
> He in ful purpos to yeue* it to the kyng. *give
>
> (I, 186–92)[4]

That is, Curteys conceived the idea of Lydgate undertaking a translation 'out of the latyn' as a way of commemorating the king's visit so that Curteys could present it to Henry ('yeve it to the kyng'). Lydgate seems to have begun his task hard upon Henry's departure from Bury. As he says,

> Whan I first gan on this translacion:
> Yt was the yeer by computacion,
> Whan sixte Herry in his estat roial
> With his sceptre of Yngland and of France
> Heeld at Bury the feste pryncipal* *chief feast
> Of Cristemesse with ful gret habundance,
> And aftir that list to haue plesance* — **wished to have the pleasure*
> As his consail* gan for him prouide* *counsellors *prepared for him*
> There in his place til hesterne* for to abide: *Easter
>
> (I, 135–43)

What makes the plan particularly appropriate is the nature of the translation with which Lydgate was charged. This is announced in the opening lines:

> The noble story to putte in remembrance
> Of saynt Edmund, martir maide, & kyng,
> With his support my stile I wil auance*: *address
> First to compile aftir my kunyng* **according to my ability*
> His glorious lif . . .
>
> (I, 81–5)

Henry's visit was to be commemorated by a life of the Anglo-Saxon king, St Edmund. It was an entirely fitting, and extremely astute gesture. Edmund was the patron saint of the Abbey. Long before Lydgate's time Bury was firmly established as a site for those wishing to venerate the saint. In a short, separately composed prayer to St Edmund, Lydgate reports that Edmund's 'hooly nailles' and 'royal heer / . . . be conserved yit in thyn hooly place, / With other relyques, ffor a memoryall' and he exhorts the saint to ' . . . pray for all that kome on pilgrimage / From euery party of this regioun.'[5]

---

[4] Quotations from Lydgate's poem are from the edition by Carl Horstmann, 'S. Edmund und Fremund', in *Altenglische Legenden*, Neue Folge (Heilbronn, 1881), pp. 376–440. Book and line references are given parenthetically in the text. Occasionally Horstmann's transcription has been silently corrected.

[5] John Lydgate, 'St Edmund', *The Minor Poems of John Lydgate*, ed. H. N. MacCracken, Early English Text Society, extra series 107 (London: Oxford University Press, 1911), pp. 124–7.

The presentation of Lydgate's verse life to Henry VI was a deft move. The twelve-year-old king was already demonstrating the profound religious piety that was to be one of his most consistent attributes throughout his life.[6] In this respect Lydgate's poem drew an implicit parallel between Henry and an earlier equally devout king. It also made a more direct connection between the origins of this prominent royally founded religious house, its present status, and its hope of future protection under kingly favour.

The Poet

If the *Lives of SS Edmund and Fremund* was most likely the brainchild of William Curteys, then John Lydgate was the inevitable choice to implement it because of his long and close association with the Abbey at Bury and his status as the preeminent English poet of the fifteenth century.[7]

Lydgate had been born *c.*1370 in the village of Lydgate in Suffolk. While still a child he entered the monastery at Bury St Edmunds and was ordained priest there in 1397. He subsequently studied at Oxford. While there he seems to have gained the support of the Prince of Wales, the future Henry V. It was under Henry's auspices that he wrote his first major poem, the *Troy Book*, composed between *c.*1412 and 1420, a lengthy history of the Trojan legend. He also wrote, with Henry's encouragement, his *Life of Our Lady*, a widely popular life of the Virgin Mary. For a period in the 1420s he was employed in royal service in France.

These works, among others, served to establish Lydgate's poetic reputation and led to an extraordinarily diverse series of literary commissions. He wrote poems in a remarkable variety of kinds at the request of a range of individuals and institutions. These works extended from historical works to saints' lives to courtly verse to dramatic texts to political propaganda to prayers; they even included a treatise for laundresses and a verse dietary. If the number and often the quality of surviving manuscripts are secure guides, many of these works had a wide contemporary appeal.

By the early 1430s, in his early sixties, Lydgate had returned to the Abbey at Bury St Edmunds, where he largely remained until his death. It is to the beginning of this final period of his life that the composition of his *Lives of SS Edmund and Fremund* belongs. Lydgate undertook it even though he was in the middle of his longest and most ambitious poem, *The Fall of Princes* (it runs to over 36,000 lines), a series of secular verse tragedies of famous men, composed between 1431 and 1438 at the request of Humfrey, Duke of Gloucester. But the exhortation of his Abbot

---

[6] It is the quality emphasized most consistently by his first biographer, John Blacman; see the edition by M. R. James (Cambridge: Cambridge University Press, 1921), pp. 4–22; for modern discussion see Ralph A. Griffiths, *The Reign of Henry VI* (London: Benn, 1981), pp. 248–9.

[7] For the most recent account of Lydgate's life see Derek Pearsall, *John Lydgate (1371–1449): A Bio-Bibliography*, English Literary Studies Monograph Series, No. 71 (Victoria, B.C.: University of Victoria, 1997).

was one that Lydgate would have found impossible to resist. As he implies in his preamble to the poem, the commission was probably issued immediately after Henry's visit. In view of his apparent facility in composition it was not likely to have taken him long to compose his poem. One might guess that a work of just over 3,700 lines would not have taken him more than a year, even allowing for his other commitments. Indeed, age seems to have done little to lessen Lydgate's fluency of composition; he continued to produce verse until virtually the moment of his death in 1449.

The Poem

If occasion, place and poet all have their peculiar appropriateness to Lydgate's *Lives of SS Edmund and Fremund*, so also does genre. The poem is a saint's life, an appropriate form in which to celebrate a famous East Anglian martyr for the first time in English verse. It is written largely in rhyme royal stanzas, a verse form that probably reflects Chaucer's influence on Lydgate. Chaucer was the first to employ it in his *Canterbury Tales* for religious or hagiographic narratives. It was the verse form Lydgate used for all his major saints' lives and for most of his other longer late poems.

The poem recounts the life and martyrdom of the East Anglian King Edmund, killed by Danish invaders in 870 at the age of twenty-nine. It also recounts the life of Fremund, son of Edmund's sister Bothild, as well as various miracles associated with St Edmund.

Lydgate's poem is divided into three Books. The narrative can be summarized as follows:

BOOK I: This recounts the birth of Edmund to Siware and Alkmund, King of Saxony. As a child he impresses Offa, King of East Anglia, (not to be confused with the actual King Offa of Mercia), who makes him his heir. As Offa lies dying, Edmund sails to East Anglia where his arrival is heralded by miraculous signs. He is crowned king and his reputation as a just and virtuous ruler spreads widely.

BOOK II: Edmund's reputation comes to the ears of Lothbrok, pagan King of Denmark. One day his boat is blown from Denmark to the Norfolk coast, where he is invited to stay by Edmund. But while hunting he is murdered by Bern, the king's huntsman. Bern is condemned and cast to sea. His boat arrives in Denmark where he tells Lothbrok's sons Hingwar and Ubba that Edmund murdered their father. They invade England, causing great slaughter, but are defeated in East Anglia by Edmund. He, however, deplores the destruction of battle and vows to fight no more. Hingwar and Ubba demand his surrender. Edmund refuses and is seized and martyred by being shot full of arrows and then decapitated. The head is hidden by a wolf. After a search the head is found and miraculously made whole with the rest of Edmund's body.

BOOK III: This is initially concerned with Edmund's cousin, Fremund, King Offa's son. Miraculous portents attend his birth and as an adult he converts the people of Mercia to Christianity. Although he sought a contemplative life on an island retreat, he is required by Offa to return and avenge Edmund's death. With twenty-four companions he routs a Danish army of 40,000 men. He is then murdered by one of his own people, Duke Oswy, who beheads him while he is at prayer. His corpse performed many miracles after his death.

The recounting of Fremund's miracles is followed by details of further miracles associated with St Edmund, including the killing of the Danish King Sven and of Sheriff Leofstan. The narrative ends with an account of the creation of a new church at Bury St Edmunds that was completed in 1095 during the administration of Abbot Baldwin (1065–97) and was to serve as a shrine to Edmund.

Lydgate's poem was clearly a popular one. Twelve manuscripts of the complete text survive as well as a number of selections or fragments,[8] some made in the sixteenth century by the famous antiquary, John Stow.[9] Several of these manuscripts, notably British Library MS Yates Thompson 47 and the Arundel Castle manuscript are very elaborately decorated with cycles of miniatures, which, although fewer in number, seemingly are derived from Harley 2278.[10] The poem also appears in a number of larger compilations, several – like those in British Library MS Harley 7333 and Manchester, Chetham's Library MS 6709 – associated with religious houses or individual religious.[11] In the 1440s Lydgate added some additional miracles to create an enlarged version of his narrative that is found in some manuscripts.[12] Clearly the patron saint of his religious house continued to engage Lydgate's imagination after his original commission had been completed. The evident contemporary popularity of his poem has been echoed in subsequent critical opinion that has also found much to admire in it.[13]

---

[8] The other manuscripts are detailed in the Bibliography; it is no. 3440 in Julia Boffey and A. S. G. Edwards, *A New Index of Middle English Verse* (London: British Library, 2005).

[9] See further, A. S. G. Edwards and J. I. Miller, 'Stow and Lydgate's *St. Edmund*', *Notes and Queries*, 228 (1973), 365–9.

[10] For discussion of these manuscripts and their illustrations see Kathleen L. Scott, 'Lydgate's Lives of Saints Edmund and Fremund: A newly located manuscript in Arundel Castle', *Viator*, 13 (1982), 335–66.

[11] Harley 7333 was in the library of Augustinian friars at St Mary le Pratis, Leicestershire; for description and discussion see J. M. Manly and E. Rickert, *The Text of the Canterbury Tales*, 8 vols (Chicago: University of Chicago Press, 1940), I, 207–218. Chetham's 6709 was owned by William Cotson, canon of the Augustinian Priory, Dunstable; see Manly and Rickert, I, 82–4 and N. R. Ker, *Medieval Manuscripts in British Libraries III: Lampeter–Oxford* (Oxford: Clarendon Press, 1983), pp. 345–7.

[12] The additional legends are printed from Bodleian Library MS Ashmole 46 in Horstmann, pp. 440–5.

[13] Modern assessments of the legend include: Walter F. Schirmer, *John Lydgate*, pp. 162–6; Th. Wolpers, *Die englische Heiligenlegende des Mittelalters*, Buchreihe der Anglia Zeitschrift für englische Philologie, Bd. 10 (Tübingen: Max Niemeyer, 1964), pp. 316–22; Derek Pearsall, *John Lydgate* (London: Routledge, 1970), pp. 280–83; J. I. Miller, Jr, 'Lydgate the Hagiographer as Literary Artist', in *The Lerned and the Lewed*. L. D. Benson, ed. (Cambridge, MA: Harvard University Press, 1974), pp. 279–90.

The Legends

The narrative of Lydgate's poem is an elaborate one, in which, in particular, Edmund's saintly status is demonstrated by a wealth of illustrative, authenticating detail. Lydgate characterizes his *Lives of SS Edmund and Fremund* as a 'translacion' (I, 135, 205; see also I, 94, 134, 190). This clearly indicates his indebtedness to some written source or sources. But the materials on which he could have drawn for his accounts, particularly of St Edmund, are the outcome of a lengthy process of amplification of the saint's life, extending over several centuries. The history of this amplification is complex and can only be outlined here.[14]

The earliest record of St Edmund is found in *The Anglo-Saxon Chronicle* (composed about 890) for 870, which gives the following brief report:

> In this year the raiding army rode across Mercia into East Anglia, and took up winter quarters at Thetford. And that winter King Edmund fought against them, and the Danes had the victory, and killed the king, and conquered all the land.[15]

It is from this kernel of historical fact that all subsequent accounts of the life of St Edmund were amplified. This is, indeed, all that is known about Edmund from near-contemporary accounts. This record is repeated in Asser's life of King Alfred (893). It was subsequently elaborated in an account by Abbo of Fleury, who more than a century after Edmund's death, between 985 and 987, composed a *Passio sancti Eadmundi*, a narrative he claims to have heard recounted by Archbishop Dunstan of Canterbury, who said that he had been told it by an aged eyewitness to Edmund's death when Dunstan himself was a young man.[16] This offers a much enlarged account of Edmund's life, and might have some tenuous historical basis given Abbo's claims about Dunstan's first-hand source. Abbo's account does not include any mention of Edmund's battle against and defeat by Hingwar, but does have a lengthy description of his martyrdom that accords with Lydgate's. Abbo's *Passio* was translated, with only minor alterations, into Old English in the late tenth century by Aelfric, Abbot of Eynsham.

The next significant recounting of Edmund's life was post-Conquest and in a different language. It is in Geoffrey Gaimar's Anglo-Norman French *L'Estoire des Engleis* and expands Abbo's account with another source that for the first time

---

[14] For the best concise accounts of the legend see Grant Loomis, 'The Growth of the St Edmund Legend', *Harvard Studies and Notes in Philology, Language and Literature*, 14 (1932), 83–113 and Dorothy Whitelock, 'Fact and Fiction in the Legend of St. Edmund', *Proceedings of the Suffolk Institute of Archaeology*, 31 (1969), 217–33.

[15] Dorothy Whitelock, ed., *The Anglo-Saxon Chronicle. A Revised Translation* (London, 1961), p. 46. Some manuscripts of the *Chronicle* specify that the Danish leaders were Hingwar and Ubba.

[16] For a modern edition of Abbo's life see M. Winterbottom, ed., *Three Lives of English Saints* (Toronto: University of Toronto Press, 1972), pp. 67–87.

does describe a battle by Edmund against the invading Danes as appears in Lydgate's narrative.

The contours of Edmund's early life are first filled out in Geoffrey de Fontibus's *Liber de infantia sancti Eadmundi*,[17] written probably in the mid-twelfth century. This gives such details as the names of his parents, Alkmund and Siwara (cf. I, 236, 272), his birthplace (Nuremberg; cf. I, 331) and describes his predecessor as King of East Anglia, Offa, his uncle. Geoffrey also reports other details that appear in Lydgate's poem: among others, the gift of a ring by Offa to Edmund (I, 525); the woman in Rome who saw a light shining from Alkmund's breast before Edmund's birth (I, 664–68).

The next version of the Edmund legend is that by Roger of Wendover in his *Chronicle*, composed in the early thirteenth century.[18] This presents an account of the significant events of Book II of Lydgate's narrative, the Danish invasion of East Anglia and Edmund's martyrdom. It describes the involuntary departure of the Danish King Lothbrok from his homeland, his hospitable reception in East Anglia by Edmund and his subsequent murder by Bern, the king's huntsman. It goes on to describe Bern's banishment by being set adrift in a boat, his arrival in Denmark and his interrogation by Lothbrok's two sons, Hinguar and Ubba, and his placing of the blame for Lothbrok's murder on Edmund (II, 106–294). The sons believe this story and sail to England. They are initially defeated by Edmund, but subsequently, to avoid further bloodshed, Edmund surrenders himself to martyrdom.

These narratives are those that are most relevant to Lydgate's version of St Edmund's life and reflect the gradual elaboration of that life over several centuries. It is unclear whether Lydgate knew these separate versions directly or had access to them through some subsequent compilation. One of the largest collections of materials on the saint (it runs to over 900 pages), is a late-fourteenth-century manuscript that is now Oxford, Bodleian Library MS Bodley 240, a manuscript that was in the library of the Abbey at Bury St Edmunds. This includes a 'Vita et Passio ... Sancti Edmundi' which Lydgate may have consulted while preparing his own life;[19] but there were other surviving accounts of its patron saint in the Abbey from which he could have drawn further information.[20] The question of Lydgate's sources is one that warrants fuller investigation than it has yet received.

---

[17] For an edition see T. Arnold, ed., *Memorials of Bury St Edmund's Abbey*, I, 93–103.

[18] For an edition see H. O. Coxe, ed., *Rogeri de Wendover Chronica*, 4 vols (London: English Historical Society, 1841), I, 300–13.

[19] For extensive discussion of this manuscript see Nicholas J. Heale, 'Religious and Intellectual Interests at Bury St Edmunds Abbey at Bury and the Nature of English Benedictinism: MS Bodley 240 in Context', D. Phil thesis, Oxford, 1994.

[20] For example, the Lives of St Edmund in BL Cotton Tiberius B. ii or the Miracula S. Edmundi in New York, Pierpont Morgan Library MS 736, both of which were in the Abbey library at Bury.

What is puzzling is Lydgate's decision to conjoin his Life of St Edmund with that of St Fremund. Very little is known about Fremund, and indeed his 'life' may be wholly fictitious. What information there is about him dates from no earlier than the mid-thirteenth century, when Henry of Avranches composed a verse Latin life, which followed one of St Edmund. The contours of Fremund's life were established here and later accounts offer only minor expansions or omissions. But the meagre historical evidence indicates that Fremund died before Edmund, in 866; Lydgate's characterization of him as a hero who is called into action after Edmund's death seems to lack any historical basis. The motives for the inclusion of his life in Lydgate's work remain obscure. Lydgate does not mention him in his opening statement of his poem's scope (lines 1–5). It seems that the Life of Fremund was an afterthought, included for reasons that cannot be recovered. Fremund's life does offer a muted counterpoint to Edmund's, but Lydgate's version of it is quite terse and he swiftly returns to his original subject to record further miracles of St Edmund. It is Edmund who naturally forms the central concern of Lydgate's poem. As has been noted, at some point in the 1440s he produced an expanded version of his narrative including some further miracles associated with the saint. Such an expansion indicates the fluidity of the legend and the range of materials available to Lydgate in writing his life of Bury's patron saint.

The Illustrations

The Abbey at Bury was wealthy, and Lydgate was one of its members and the foremost poet of his time. It would naturally have sought to represent itself and its poet as impressively as possible in a work intended for presentation to the king. In terms of both the number and quality of its pictures, Harley 2278 is one of the most remarkable surviving illustrated manuscripts of Middle English verse in the fifteenth century.

The manuscript contains 120 illustrations. Two of these, on fols 1v and 3v, are full-page, designed to accompany the prologue (fols 1v–5). They elaborate brief allusions in the prologue, to Adam and Eve and the banner of St Edmund (fol. 1v) and to the three crowns that form the arms of the Abbey of Bury St Edmunds (fol. 3v). They are probably late additions to the manuscript and are the only full-page illustrations in it.

The remaining 118 illustrations are all closely related to the actual narratives of the lives of Saints Edmund and Fremund. This relationship is indicated in part by their integration into the text page. Forty-seven of these are approximately two stanzas in size (that is, two-thirds of the text page): they measure approximately 100 × 100 mm on average;[21] the remaining 71 are usually one stanza in size (that is,

---

[21] An exception is fol. 52 where the height of the miniature is reduced (110 × 80 mm) to accommodate a single stanza and a prose heading.

one third of the text page): approximately 100 × 50 mm on average.[22] This integration means that the pictures form a coherent visual parallel to the text of the poem and constitute as much a part of the narrative as does the text itself. Some effort has also been made to distribute them throughout the narrative; at only three points (fols 86, 93v, 97v) does more than one illustration occur on a page. There are very slight variations in the width of some of the miniatures, particularly the smaller ones. But one of the striking features of these is their use of horizontal space: even when a number of figures are laterally deployed there is no sense of clutter or of inert deployment; their disposition reflects a sense of movement and space (see, for example, fols 18v, 19, 22, 22v, 25, 25v, 26, 27v, 28v, 29, 29v, 30, 47v). At times, the crowded but varied nature of the composition works actually to enact the activity being represented, as in the miniature of the building of the 'roial toun' (I, 768) on fol. 28v, or of the battle at Thetford (fol. 50). Only rarely is the space and activity less successfully realized, as in the rather formless battle scene on fol. 86v.

The illustrations vary in their levels of representation of the narrative. But a number do represent more than one scene within a single picture. Such 'compound' pictures occur on fols 12, 23, 41v, 42, 43v, 44, 44v, 45v, 47, 62, 67, 72, 76, 77, 80, 81, 90, 91, 102v, 107v, 110v, 112v, 115v. There are some patterns to their occurrence. For example, those on fols 41v, 42, 43v, 44, 44v, 45, 47 all relate to the life and death of Lothbrok and Bern's exile for his murder. Those on fols 76, 77, 80, 81, 90, 91 all represent the life of Fremund. And the final ones, fols 102v, 107v, 110v, 112v, 115v, all depict incidents connected with Edmund's posterity and his translation to Bury. Why it was felt necessary to include more than a single incident in an illustration at these points in the narrative is not altogether clear. Perhaps it was the necessary way of confining the poem's programme of illustration to the overall constraints of the manuscript's length and design. And it may also be a means of underscoring the particularly dramatic moments in the narrative. At times the compression of several incidents is particularly striking. For example, on fol. 67v we see enacted in the single miniature the recovery and restoration of Edward's missing head; here the miniature employs dual occurrences of the same figures and images to great effect: the wolf, first standing, then sitting; the monk who first finds the head then restores it to the body (his identity in both roles firmly established by the reappearance of his tonsure, his pink belt and blue collar in both images); and, of course, the head itself, first dramatically foregrounded in isolation, then shown restored to Edmund's body. Again, on fol. 110v, we see the depiction of Osgothus, 'a lord of Denmark' (III, 1245), who 'despysed his [i.e. St Edmund's] myracles whan he herde hem reede' (III, 1249); we

---

[22] There are occasional exceptions to this accommodation of miniatures within the text frame: on fol. 30 the miniature is slightly more elongated than usual (110 × 80 mm) and extends into the lower margin.

then see him reduced to the state of 'a demonyak', a madman (III, 1270), in consequence of his presumption; while 'hool al the conuent', (III, 1277), prays for him and he gives thanks for his restoration to sanity. Such visual narrative economy encompasses all the essential elements of the narrative at the appropriate point.

The pictures show a clear sense of the poem's illustrative potential and are usually carefully integrated into the actual sequence of the narrative itself, with a careful awareness of its specifics, and fidelity to them in matters of detail. The occasion when Ethelbert confronts 'the angel [who] pullid his ryht arm out off ioynt' (III, 780), is an example; the illustration shows the right arm being wrenched (fol. 96). Such fidelity is also seen, for example, in visual conformity to the poem's numerical specifications, as with the 'fyue wellis' (I, 755), that appear on Edmund's arrival in East Anglia (fol. 28), and 'the sowhe, the piggis . . . / And preestis fyue' (III, 811–12) that Ethelbertus encounters (fol. 98), as well as in other narrative elements that are incorporated into the illustration, like the rainbow that accompanied Fremund's birth (fol. 72v). Even quite complex problems of representation are tackled effectively, as, for example, on fol. 12, where an attempt is made to find a visual correlation to the description of Alkmund: 'Out of his brest a sonne shal out spreede' (I, 311). Perhaps fortunately, the ingenuity of the artist is rarely taxed to this degree elsewhere.

On occasions, the sense of visual narrative employs elements that give an extra-textual continuity to the poem itself. A case in point is Lothbrok's greyhound, a creature who, after his master's death, returns to Edmund ('In kam his grehound and fawne gan the kyng / Fil doun toforn him ful pitously whynyng' (II, 195–6), and leads the king to the corpse of his master. This is the first mention of the greyhound in the poem. But his crucial narrative function is adumbrated in his appearance in a sequence of miniatures going back to Lothbrok's departure from Denmark, on fols 41v, 42, and 43, as well as on those on fols 44, 44v and 45v which directly reflect the poem's action. There is a similar extra-textual element to the interring of the restored body of Edmund. Again, a creature is involved, this time the wolf that protected the severed head until it is found. His presence in the narrative is reflected in the relevant miniature on fols 64v and 66. But he is also seen in the margin of the miniature of the building of Edmund's 'sepulture' (II, 977) on fol. 68v, doubtless as a means of underscoring his miraculous role.

The miniatures nonetheless in general provide clear indications that the artists worked in concert with someone who had read the text attentively and wished to reflect the narrative not just in the subject matter of the illustrations but also in their careful positioning within the poem in relation to the appropriate point in the text. The correlation between text and images suggests the possibility that Lydgate himself may have been consulted about the design of the pictures.[23] The

---

[23] As is suggested by Kathleen Scott, *Later Gothic Manuscripts 1390–1490*, 2 vols (London: Harvey Miller, 1996), II, 228.

INTRODUCTION 11

intention is achieved all the more powerfully, of course, by the simple fact of the number of such illustrations. Indeed, the ratio of illustration to text is remarkably high throughout the entire narrative, averaging more than one illustration for each leaf of the manuscript. The overall effect is to create an unusually powerful synthesis in which the verbal and visual elements of the manuscript complement one another in a carefully integrated way.

It is hard to point to precedents for this degree of integration of text and image in the preparation of the fifteenth-century Middle English verse manuscripts. The famous Ellesmere manuscript of Chaucer's *Canterbury Tales* (Huntington Library MS EL 26 C 9),[24] contains marginal miniatures of the pilgrims. But these illustrations are portraits; they show no direct engagement with Chaucer's narratives. The infrequent illustrations in other *Canterbury Tales* manuscripts do not indicate any sustained effort to reflect narrative. In fact, the most substantial parallels to the scale of illustration in verse texts occur in other Lydgate manuscripts, Manchester University Library Rylands English 1, the *Troy Book*, and British Library MS Harley 1766, the *Fall of Princes*, as well as in the other illustrated copies of the *Lives of SS Edmund and Fremund* in British Library MS Yates Thompson 47 and the Arundel Castle manuscript.[25]

The scale of illustrative ambition in the manuscript clearly involved the recruitment of considerable artistic resources. The hands of at least three artists have been distinguished in the manuscript's pictures.[26] Apportioning their respective roles in the manuscript's illustration is not always easy, and it is possible that more than one artist may have worked on the same miniature. The principal artist appears to have had two different assistants, one helping with most of the miniatures in the first half of the manuscript, another involved in helping only in the second half of it. Nothing is known about the identities of these artists. They are often assumed to be from the Continent because of the quality of their workmanship. Certainly a number of the most distinguished artists in England in the first half of the fifteenth century were from the Continent, but such speculation about the origins of the artists in Harley 2278 cannot be confirmed.

Some stylistic attributes seem common to all three artists. They show sensitivity to detail, particularly of costume (see fols 27, 30), which is rendered throughout with a sensitivity to style and the natural folds of drapery (see, for

[24] For the most recent authoritative description of the manuscript see Consuelo Dutschke, et al., *Guide to Medieval and Renaissance Manuscripts in the Huntington Library*, 2 vols (San Marino, CA, 1989), I, 41–50; for discussion of its illustrations and full bibliography see Kathleen Scott, *Later Gothic Manuscripts*, II, 140–3.

[25] The first two of these are discussed in Scott, *Later Gothic Manuscripts*, II, 259–63 and 302–4 respectively, with full references to earlier scholarship; on the two Edmund and Fremund manuscripts see Scott, 'Lydgate's Lives of Saints Edmund and Fremund'.

[26] I follow here Scott's differentiation of the artists' stints; see *Later Gothic Manuscripts*, II, 227–8.

example, fol. 29v), as well as to armour and weaponry (see, for example, fols 42, 86). There is also a consistent concern with the representation of physical detail: faces and hands are carefully depicted (see, for example, fols 13, 17, 36, 37). The larger environments in which action is set also receive careful attention. Occasionally, domestic interiors are realized with a wealth of circumstantial detail (see, for example, fols 13v, 74). Similar attention is paid to the representation of exteriors like Offa's tomb (fol. 22v), or the pagan temple in which Lothbrok and his sons are worshipping idols (fol. 39) or the 'lytil chapel' (III, 365) Fremund built on Ilefaye.

There are some differences in the artists' practices. The artist who worked on the second part of the manuscript often seems to give rather sharper definition to both figures and buildings, and to differentiate foliage and grass more elaborately. At times the dramatization of space seems more conventional than in the earlier parts of the manuscript, as with the focus on the dismembered head of Fremund, fols 88v, 88, 90. But there some striking dramatic effects, as with the miniature of Edmund impaling Sweyn (fol. 103v).

There is no direct indication of the place of production of the manuscript. But circumstantial evidence suggests that it was very probably produced at Bury St Edmunds itself.[27] The Abbey was wealthy enough to commission talented scribes and decorators. There is also other evidence to associate the town or the Abbey with the production of elaborate manuscripts during the 1430s and 1440s. These include at least one manuscript of another of Lydgate's works, his *Fall of Princes*, that has some stylistic links to Harley 2278, and was contemporaneous with the *Lives of SS Edmund and Fremund*. The greater part of this manuscript now forms Huntington Library MS HM 268, and a fragment of which is British Library MS Sloane 2452.[28] It is also noteworthy that a further, larger group of manuscripts associated with Lydgate, all copied in the 1460s by the same scribe and sharing some of the same decorators, has also been associated with Bury St Edmunds.[29] It is possible that this group of manuscripts was produced to satisfy an established local interest in the writings of a poet who recurrently characterized himself as 'monk of Bury'.

What is unclear, either in relation to Harley 2278 or these later manuscripts, is whether the Abbey possessed its own scriptorium that regularly produced a variety of manuscripts for its own use and for wealthy local collectors, or whether it hired

---

[27] Harley 2278 would then provide a rare instance of direct collaboration between poet and artists in the creation of a manuscript.

[28] See further, Scott, *Later Gothic Manuscripts*, II, 229–31, for a description of the Huntington manuscript's decoration and its relationship to Harley 2278; see also A. S. G. Edwards, 'The Huntington *Fall of Princes* and Sloane 2452', *Manuscripta*, 16 (1972), 380–5.

[29] On this group see A. S. G. Edwards, 'The McGill Fragment of Lydgate's *Fall of Princes*', *Scriptorium*, 28 (1974), 75–7, and Kathleen L. Scott, 'Lydgate's Lives of Saints Edmund and Fremund', 335–66.

scribes and artists on an *ad hoc* basis to execute particular commissions. What is evident is that whatever agency or agencies were involved had access, in the preparation of Harley 2278, to a range of artistic resources that enabled the production of one of the most remarkable manuscripts of its age. The overall scale and quality of the illustration and decoration justifies the consensus of art historians that it is among the greatest pieces of East Anglian manuscript production in the fifteenth century.

The Manuscript

British Library MS Harley 2278 is a manuscript of 119 parchment leaves. Each leaf measures approximately 250 × 170 mm. The text is contained within a ruled frame 140 × 110 mm, into which the text and, where it occurs, miniature and/or occasionally (for example fols 16, 31v) headings are accommodated.

The manuscript is largely in quires of eight leaves, with the exception of the first and last quires. Its collation can be expressed thus: $[1]^6$ (lacking the final leaf, which was almost certainly blank), $a-o^8$, p^2; that is, there is an initial unsigned gathering of six leaves, lacking the last leaf; fourteesn quires of eight leaves, and a final quire of two leaves. Most of the gatherings have quire signatures and there are regular catchwords. It is copied by a single scribe in a rather angular semi-cursive hand, writing in a Suffolk dialect.[30]

The anomalous nature of the first, unsigned gathering suggests that it may have been a late addition to the manuscript. Although the scribe seems to be the same as in the main text, the style of decoration and illustration is different, particularly in the two full-page miniatures that occur (there are none in the main text). These prefatory verses were doubtless added at the final stages in the manuscript's preparation to record formally Henry VI's visit to Bury and Abbot Curteys's desire to commemorate it through Lydgate's poem.

Harley 2278 contains a single verse text, a copy of John Lydgate's *Lives of SS Edmund and Fremund*. The main text of the poem, in seven-line, rhyme royal stanzas, is laid out with one-line spaces between each stanza. The layout of fols 2–4v and 117–118v, where Lydgate wrote in eight-line stanzas, is rather more cramped than elsewhere in the manuscript since there was not room to leave space between stanzas. Throughout the manuscript the text is copied to ensure that each page ends with a complete stanza.

In addition to its illustrations (discussed above) the manuscript contains occasional elaborate demi-vinet borders (that is, a two-or-three-sided border) on fols 6 and 10v, the latter incorporating an image of David fighting a dragon. There are

---

[30] For some discussion of the scribe and the characteristics of his hand see C. E. Wright, *English Vernacular Hands from the Twelfth to the Fifteenth Centuries* (Oxford: Clarendon Press, 1960), p. 18; on the dialect see A. McIntosh et al., *A Linguistic Atlas of Later Middle English*, 4 vols (Aberdeen: Aberdeen University Press, 1986), III, 489–90.

some large gilt initials with foliate decoration on fols 1, 4, 4v, 5, 6 (incorporating the royal arms), 118v, 119v. There are also a large number of other gilt initials of varying sizes at the beginning of stanzas, usually infilled in blue and white vinework on a purple ground, again with white vinework and gold and green sprays; sometimes the colours are alternated or quartered. Most of the other initials at the beginning of each stanza have quite elaborate penwork flourishing. It is clear that considerable effort was expended to ensure that even those pages that were un-illustrated were visually pleasing in their level of enhancement of the text.

The elaborateness of the manuscript supports the general opinion that it was made for presentation to the young Henry VI. The miniatures include depictions of Henry kneeling at St Edmund's tomb (fol. 4v) and the presentation of a book, doubtless the work itself, to the king (fol. 6). The quality of its production clearly indicates that the manuscript would have taken some time to prepare after Lydgate had completed the composition of the poem. Since Lydgate began to receive a royal pension in 1439,[31] it is tempting – and reasonable – to suppose that this reward was an acknowledgement of Henry's receipt of this manuscript. Hence, the *Lives of SS Edmund and Fremund* was probably composed, and the presentation copy that is now Harley 2278 completed, during the period 1434–39.

Henry would doubtless have found the manuscript particularly appealing. He owned a number of books, some in English, some clearly presentation copies like Harley 2278.[32] The manuscript seems to have remained in the royal library after his deposition and/or death. At one point, a prayer by Lydgate to Henry has been erased and replaced by one to Edward IV, his successor.[33] And at some point after this, the manuscript appears to have left royal hands. On fol. 119v there is an inscription 'Audelay baron', the signature of John Touchet, 8th Baron Audley (d. 1559). Since the book is included in inventories of the library of Henry VIII it would seem that Audley presented it to the king in the early sixteenth century, probably c.1512 in gratitude for his restoration to rank and title.[34] Subsequently it left the royal collection and nothing is known of its history before the early eighteenth century when it entered the Harley library.[35] It

---

[31] For details of this grant see Pearsall, *John Lydgate (1371–1449): A Bio-Bibliography*, pp. 59–60.

[32] For details of some of these see J. J. G. Alexander, 'Painting and Manuscript Illumination in the Later Middle Ages', in *English Court Culture in the Later Middle Ages*, ed. V. J. Scattergood and J. W. Sherborne (London: Duckworth, 1983), pp. 150–2.

[33] The deletion occurs on fol. 98; the original reading 'saue sixte Herry' is replaced by 'saue forthe Edward' (Horstmann, p. 428, line 833 and note).

[34] See further, James P. Carley, *The Libraries of King Henry VIII* (London: British Library, 2000), xlviii.

[35] On 16 August, 1720, obtained from a 'Mr Colston'; see C. E. and R. C. Wright, eds, *The Diary of Humfrey Wanley, 1715–1726*, 2 vols (London: The Bibliographical Society, 1966), I, 64. The manuscript does have on a flyleaf, the early eighteenth-century initials 'Mrs DL' but the name cannot be identified; see C. E. Wright, *Fontes Harleianae* (London: British Museum, 1972), pp. 110, 122.

passed with the rest of the manuscripts in that library to the British Museum in 1753 and thence to the British Library.[36]

[36] In the late eighteenth century the manuscript was examined by the Danish Old English scholar, Gunnur Jonsson Thorklelin, who had an illustrated copy of it prepared; this is now Copenhagen, Royal Library MS N. k. s. 513[b]; see further Kevin S. Kiernan, 'Thorkelin's Trip to Great Britain and Ireland, 1786–1791', *The Library*, 6th ser., 5 (1983), 1–21.

BIBLIOGRAPHY

Manuscripts of Lydgate's Lives of SS Edmund and Fremund (apart from Harley 2278):

Oxford, Bodleian Library, Ashmole 46 (SC 6930), fols 1–96

Oxford, Bodleian Library, Tanner 347 (SC 10174), fols 1–86v

Oxford, Bodleian Library, Rawl. B.216 (SC 11568), fols 162v–71v

Oxford, Corpus Christi College 61, fols 1–63, 65v–66

Cambridge, University Library, Ee.2.15, fols 48–102v

London, British Library, Harley 372, fols 1–43

London, British Library, Harley 4826, fols 4–44, 45v–46

London, British Library, Harley 7333, fols 136–46v

London, British Library, Yates Thompson 47 (*olim* Mostyn 84), pp. 1–213

Manchester, Chetham's Library 6709, fols 199–282v

Arundel Castle manuscript (s.n.), fols 1–99

There are extracts or fragments in:

Oxford, Bodleian Library, Ashmole 59 (SC 6943), fol. 23v (a single envoy in the hand of the fifteenth-century scribe, John Shirley)

London, British Library, Harley 367, fol. 86v (a single envoy in a sixteenth-century copy by the antiquary, John Stow)

London, British Library, Harley 247, fol. 45 (a brief extract)

Exeter, Devon County Record Office Misc. Roll 59 (fragment; printed in Clarke; see Bibliography below)

Other Primary Works

Arnold, T., ed., *Memorials of Bury St Edmund's Abbey*. 3 vols. London: Rolls Series, 189–96.

Blacman, John, *Henry the Sixth, A Reprint of John Blacman's Memoir*. Ed. with translation and notes by M. R. James. Cambridge: Cambridge University Press, 1921.

Coxe, H. O., ed., *Rogeri de Wendover Chronica*. 4 vols. London: English Historical Society, 1841.

Hervey, Lord Francis, ed., *Corolla Sancti Eadmundi: The Garland of St Edmund, King and Martyr*. London: John Murray, 1907.

Lydgate, John, *The Minor Poems of John Lydgate*. Ed. H. N. MacCracken, Early English Text Society, extra series 107. London: Oxford University Press, 1911.

―― *Lydgate's Fall of Princes*. Ed. H. Bergen, 4 vols, Early English Text Society, extra series, 121–24. London: Oxford University Press, 1924–27.

―― 'S. Edmund und Fremund'. *Altenglische Legenden*. Neue Folge. Ed. Carl Horstmann. Heilbronn, 1881.

Wanley, Humfrey, *The Diary of Humfrey Wanley, 1715–1726*. Ed. C. E. and R. C. Wright, 2 vols. London: The Bibliographical Society, 1966.

Winterbottom, M., ed., *Three Lives of English Saints*. Toronto: University of Toronto Press, 1972.

Secondary Works

Alexander, J. J. G., 'Painting and Manuscript Illumination in the Later Middle Ages'. *English Court Culture in the Later Middle Ages*. Ed. V. J. Scattergood and J. W. Sherborne. London: Duckworth, 1983. Pp. 141–62.

Carley, James P., *The Libraries of King Henry VIII*. London: British Library, 2000.

Clarke, D. E. M., 'A New Lydgate Manuscript'. *Modern Language Review*, 24 (1929), 324–8.

Edwards, A. S. G., 'The Huntington *Fall of Princes* and Sloane 2452'. *Manuscripta*, 16 (1972), 380–5.

―― 'The McGill Fragment of Lydgate's *Fall of Princes*'. *Scriptorium*, 28 (1974), 75–7.

―― and J. I. Miller, 'Stow and Lydgate's *St Edmund*'. *Notes and Queries*, 228 (1973), 365–9.

Griffiths, Ralph A., *The Reign of Henry VI*. London: Benn, 1981.

Heale, Nicholas J., 'Religious and Intellectual Interests at Bury St Edmunds Abbey at Bury and the Nature of English Benedictinism: MS Bodley 240 in Context'. D. Phil thesis, Oxford, 1994.

Kiernan, Kevin S., 'Thorkelin's Trip to Great Britain and Ireland, 1786–1791'. *The Library*, 6th ser., 5 (1983), 1–21.

Loomis, Grant, 'The Growth of the St Edmund Legend'. *Harvard Studies and Notes in Philology, Language and Literature*, 14 (1932), 83–113.

Manly, J. M. and E. Rickert, *The Text of the Canterbury Tales*, 8 vols. Chicago: University of Chicago Press, 1940.

McIntosh, A. et al., *A Linguistic Atlas of Later Middle English*, 4 vols. Aberdeen: Aberdeen University Press, 1986.

McKeehan, Irene P., 'St Edmund of Anglia: The Development of a Romantic Legend'. *University of Colorado Studies*, General Series 15 (1925), 13–74.

Miller, James I., Jr., 'Literature to History: Exploring a Medieval Saint's Legend and its Context'. *University of Tulsa Monograph Series*, 9 (1970). Pp. 59–72.

―― 'Lydgate the Hagiographer as Literary Artist'. *The Lerned and the Lewed*. Ed. L. D. Benson. Cambridge, MA: Harvard University Press, 1974. Pp. 279–90.

—— and A. S. G. Edwards, 'Stow and Lydgate's *St. Edmund*'. *Notes and Queries*, 228 (1973), 365–9.

Ord, Craven, 'Account of the Entertainment of King Henry the Sixth at the Abbey of Bury St Edmunds'. *Archaeologia*, 15 (1806), 65–71.

Pearsall, Derek, *John Lydgate*. London: Routledge, 1970.

—— *John Lydgate (1371–1449): A Bio-Bibliography*. English Literary Studies Monograph Series, No. 71. Victoria, B. C.: University of Victoria, 1997.

Schirmer, Walter F., *John Lydgate, A Study in the Culture of the XVth Century*. Tr. Ann E. Keep. London: Methuen, 1961.

Scott, Kathleen L., *Later Gothic Manuscripts, 1390–1490*. 2 vols. London: Harvey Miller, 1996.

—— 'Lydgate's Lives of Saints Edmund and Fremund: A Newly Located Manuscript in Arundel Castle'. *Viator*, 13 (1982), 335–66.

Whitelock, Dorothy, 'Fact and Fiction in the Legend of St. Edmund'. *Proceedings of the Suffolk Institute of Archaeology*, 31 (1969), 217–33.

Wolpers, Th., *Die englische Heiligenlegende des Mittelalters*. Buchreihe der Anglia Zeitschrift für englische Philologie, Bd. 10. Tübingen: Max Niemeyer, 1964.

Wright, C. E., *Fontes Harleianae*. London: British Museum, 1972.

THE ILLUSTRATIONS

Those miniatures marked with an asterisk (*) are larger, equivalent to approximately two stanzas of text space; the others occupy approximately one stanza. For a fuller account of the illustrations in this manuscript see Kathleen L. Scott, *Later Gothic Manuscripts, 1390–1490*, 2 vols (London: Harvey Miller, 1996), II, 225–6.

fol. 1v	Full-page miniature of Banner of St Edmund, Adam and Eve and Tree of Knowledge.
fol. 3v	Full-page miniature of three crowns: the arms of Abbey of Bury St Edmunds.
*fol. 4v	The young Henry VI kneeling at St Edmund's tomb.
*fol. 6	Book being presented to Henry VI.
fol. 9	Lydgate praying at St Edmund's shrine.
*fol. 10	King Alkmund and Queen Siware.
fol. 11v	Alkmund greeting Siware.
*fol. 12	Alkmund with sun shining from his heart and then kneeling before Pope.
*fol. 13	Return of Alkmund.
*fol. 13v	Birth of St Edmund.
*fol. 16v	Offa, King of East Anglia, on board ship.
fol. 17	Offa landing in Saxony.
fol. 18v	Offa meeting Edmund.
fol. 19	Offa giving ring to Edmund.
fol. 20	Offa's departure.
fol. 20v	Offa kneeling at the holy sepulchre.
fol. 21	Offa on his deathbed.
fol. 22	Offa's funeral.
*fol. 22v	Offa's burial.

*fol. 23	Alkmund receiving news of Offa's death and giving ring to Edmund.
*fol. 24	Alkmund's lords in council.
*fol. 25	Alkmund and Edmund in court.
*fol. 25v	Alkmund choosing clerks.
fol. 26	Edmund's departure.
*fol. 27	Edmund departing onboard a ship.
*fol. 27v	Edmund arriving in England.
fol. 28	Edmund praying; appearance of five wells.
fol. 28v	Edmund supervising building of Hunstanton.
fol. 29	Edmund holding court.
fol. 29v	Bishop Kunbertus in a crowd, showing Offa's ring.
*fol. 30	Edmund journeying to Bury St Edmunds.
*fol. 31	Edmund's coronation.
*fol. 32	Edmund in his court.
fol. 34	Edmund on his throne.
fol. 36	Edmund hearing pleas in his court.
*fol. 37	Edmund engaging in kingly sports.
*fol. 39	Lothbrok and his sons worshipping idols.
fol. 41v	Lothbrok boarding a boat with his hounds and then at sea.
fol. 42	Lothbrok landing in Norfolk and being received by Edmund.
fol. 43v	Lothbrok hunting.
fol. 44	Lothbrok murdered by Bern and his body concealed.
fol. 44v	Lothbrok's hound returning to Edmund's court.
fol. 45v	Hound leading knight to discovery of Lothbrok's body.
fol. 46	Bern being cast adrift.
fol. 47	Bern arriving in Denmark.
fol. 47v	Hyngwar and Ubba setting out with their navy.
fol. 48	Danes engaging in destruction.

THE ILLUSTRATIONS

21

fol. 48v	English submitting to Danes.
fol. 50	Edmund defeating Hyngwar.
*fol. 52	Hyngwar sending messenger to Edmund.
fol. 52v	Edmund receiving message.
fol. 54	Edmund consulting with a bishop.
fol. 55v	Edmund talking to a bishop.
fol. 56v	Edmund speaking to a messenger.
fol. 58	Messenger kneeling before Hyngwar.
fol. 58v	Edmund and Hyngwar.
fol. 60v	Edmund being beaten.
fol. 61	Edmund's martyrdom.
*fol. 62	Edmund being removed from the tree.
*fol. 63	Edmund being beheaded.
fol. 63v	The hiding of Edmund's head.
fol. 64	The wolf guarding Edmund's head.
*fol. 65	Christians seeking Edmund's head.
*fol. 66	The finding of Edmund's head.
*fol. 67v	The restoration of Edmund's head to his body.
*fol. 68v	Burial of Edmund in his tomb.
fol. 72	Fremund's birth.
*fol. 72v	Rainbow at Fremund's birth.
fol. 74	Burchard writing.
*fol. 75	Aldare and his wife.
fol. 76	Thoua's baptism and Fremund's birth.
*fol. 77	Birth and christening of Fremund.
*fol. 79	Fremund's coronation.
fol. 79v	Fremund departing for a desert island.
*fol. 80	Fremund's journey to (and arrival on) the island.

*fol. 81	Fremund at prayer and work.
*fol. 82v	Messengers being sent to seek Fremund.
fol. 83	Messengers arriving and meeting Fremund.
fol. 84v	Fremund praying.
*fol. 85	Angel appearing to Fremund.
fol. 85v	Fremund returning to Mercia by ship.
fol. 86	Hyngwar sending herald to Fremund.
fol. 86	Herald before Fremund.
*fol. 86v	Fremund defeating the Danes.
fol. 87v	Fremund giving thanks for victory.
fol. 88	Oswy beheading Fremund.
fol. 88v	Oswy repenting next to Fremund's body.
*fol. 89	Fremund's head speaking to Oswy.
*fol. 90	Fremund's miraculous acts.
fol. 90v	Fremund dying.
fol. 91	Fremund's body being taken for burial.
*fol. 91v	Three virgins.
fol. 92	Three virgins travelling.
*fol. 92v	Virgins removing Fremund's corpse from tomb.
fol. 93v	Three virgins with body.
fol. 93v	Three virgins beside tree.
fol. 94	Angel speaking to virgins.
fol. 95	Edelbert praying.
fol. 96	Edelbert and an angel.
fol. 96v	Edelbert and the Pope.
*fol. 97	Edelbert near Fremund's grave with five priests.
fol. 97v	Fremund's body being carried.
fol. 97v	Pilgrims at shrine at Dunstable.

THE ILLUSTRATIONS   23

*fol. 98v   Sweyn, King of the Danes landing.

*fol. 100v   People praying at Edmund's shrine.

fol. 102v   Edmund appearing to Ailwyn; Ailwyn sending message to Sweyn.

*fol. 103v   Edmund impaling Sweyn.

fol. 105v   Sweyn on deathbed.

*fol. 106   Woman being pulled from Edmund's shrine.

fol. 107v   Leofstan dying.

*fol. 108   Knights stealing horses.

fol. 108v   Penitential knights.

fol. 109   Thief stealing jewel.

*fol. 110v   Osgoth the Dane at Edmund's tomb.

*fol. 112v   Priest's house burning and Ailwyn's entry at Cripplegate.

*fol. 113v   Removal of Edmund's tomb.

fol. 114v   Edmund's body being removed to London.

fol. 115   Edmund's body being transported.

fol. 115v   Installation of Abbot Baldwin and building of Abbey of Bury St Edmunds.

fol. 117   Edmund's remains being interred at Bury St Edmunds.

THE FACSIMILE

Oxford BH

Blyssed Edmund kyng martir and virgyne
Hadde in thre vertues by thee a souereyn prys
Which he venquysshed al venymes serpentyne
Adam baserxent banysshed fro paradys
Eua also be cause she was natt wys
Eet off an appyl off flesshly fals plesance
Which thre figures Edmund by gret auys
Bar in his baner for a remembrance

Lyk a wys kyng peeplys to gouerne
Fyrst vnto reson he gaff the souereynte
Figur off Adam wysly to dyscerne
Toppresse in Eua sensualite
A lamb off gold hyh vpon a tre
An heuenly sygne a tokne off most vertu
To declare how that humylite
Aboue alle vertues pleseth most Jhū

Off Adamys synne was wasshe away the rust
The vertu only off this lambys blood
The serpentys venym and al flesshly lust
Sathan outraied a tyran man most wood
Tyme whan this lamb was offred on the rood
For our redempcion to which hauyng reward
This hooly martir this blyssed kyng so good
Bar this lamb lift a lofte in his standard

¶ The feeld off Gothys was tokne off his suffrance
Whan cruel Danys were with hym at werre
And for a sygne off Royal suffisance
That no vices neuer maad hym erre
The feeld powdryd with many heuenly sterre
And halff cressantis off gold ful bryht and cleer
And wher that euere he iourneyde nyh or ferre
By in the feeld with hym was this baneer
¶ Which be influence off our lord Ihū
As it hath be preued offte in deede
This hooly standard hath power and vertu
To stanche fyres and stoppe flawmys rede
By myracle and who that kan take heede
God grantyd it hym for a prerogatyff
By cause al heete off lust and flesshlyheede
Were queynt in hym duryng al his lyff
¶ This vertuous baner shal kepen and conserue
This lond from enmyes daute ther cruel pryde
Off hygte Herry the noblesse to preserue
It shal be born in werrys be his syde
Tencresse his vertues Edmud shal been his guyde
By prowesse tenhance his royal lyne
This martir shal by grace for hym prouyde
To be registred amoung the worthy nyne

3

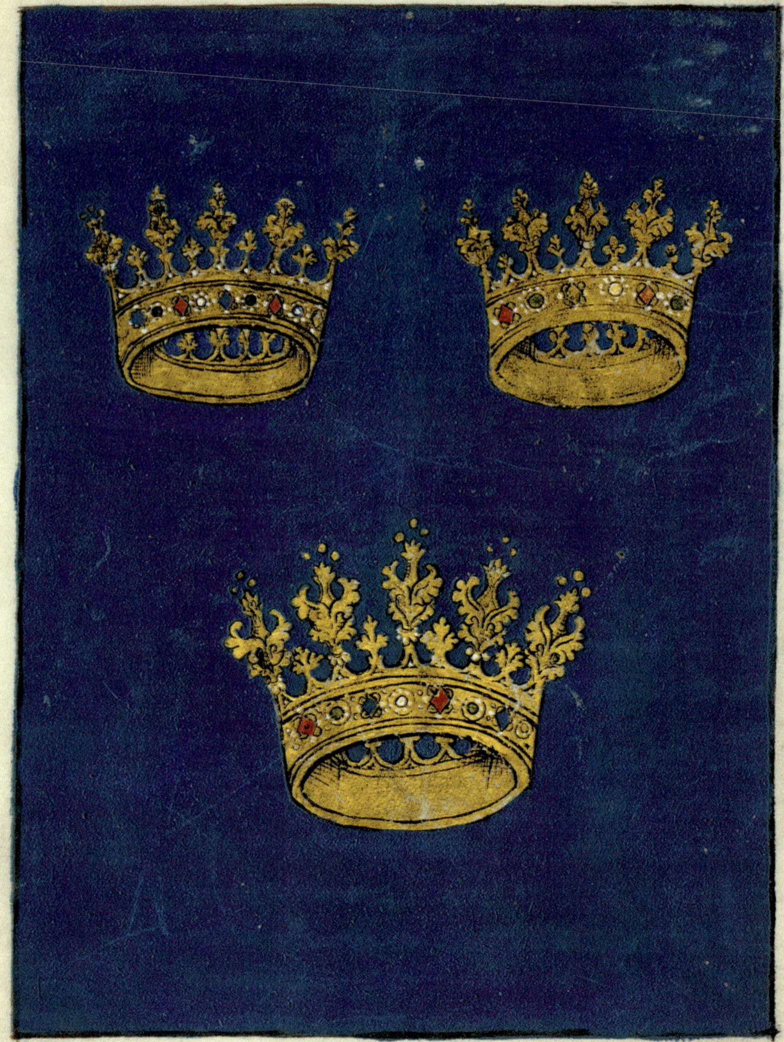

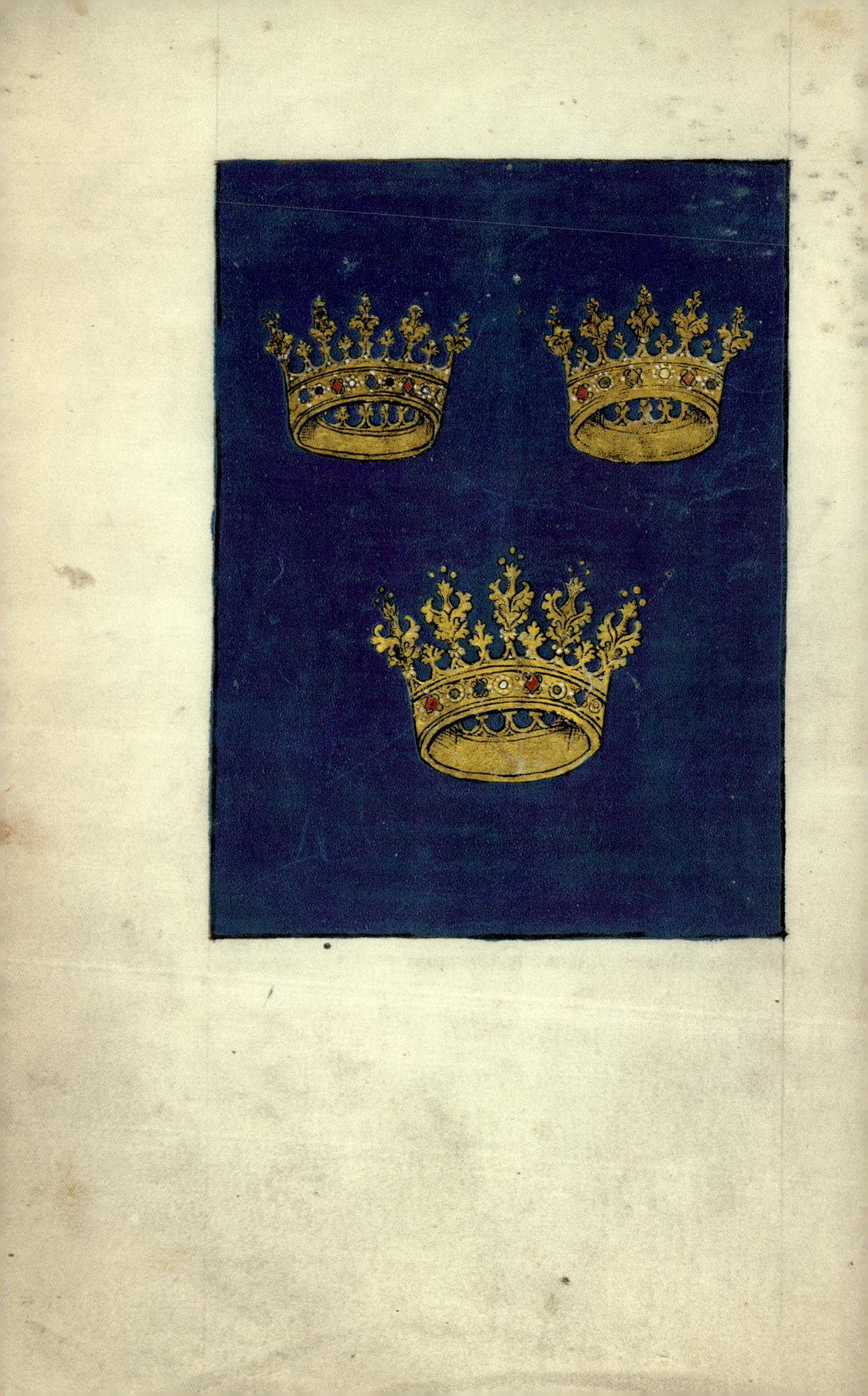

His other Standard / feeld stable off colour ynde
In which off gold / been notable crownys thre
The firste tokne / in cronycle men may fynde
Grauntyd to hym / for Royal dignyte
And the seconde / for virchynyte
ffor martirdam / the thryrde in his suffrynge
To these annexyd / fferth / hope / and charyte
In tokne he was / martyr mayde and kyng

These thre crownys / kyng Edmund bar certeyn
Whan he was sent / be grace off goddis hond
At Geynesburuh / for to slen kyng Sweyn
By which myracle / men may vndirstond
Delyuered was / fro Trybut al thys lond
That before dayes / in full notable wyse
ffor the hooly martyr / dyssolvyd hath that bond
Set this Rewm ageyn in his franchise

These thre crownys / hystoryaly taplye   Applicacio
By pronostyk / notably souereyne
To sixte Herry / in fytur sygnefye
How he is born / to worthy crownys tweyne
Off ffrance / and Ingland / lyneally atteyne
In thys lyff heer / afterward in heuene
The thryrde crowne / to receyue in certeyne
ffor his merites / a boue the sterrys seuene

O alle men, present, or in absence
Which to seynt Edmund haue deuocion
With hool herte, and deffe reuerence
Seyn this Antephne, and this Orison
Two hundred daies, ys graunted off pardoun
Wrete and registred, afforn his hooly shryne
Which for our feith, suffrede passion
Blyssyd Edmund, kyng, martir, and virgyne

Ue rex gentis anglor miles regis angelor. O
Edmunde flos martirum uelud rosa vel
lilium. funde preces ad dominum pro salute
fidelium V. Ora pro nobis beate Edmunde R. Ut
digni efficiamur promissionibus xpi. Oracio.

Deus ineffabilis misericordie qui beatissimum
Regem Edmundum tribuisti pro tui nomine
inimicum moriendo vincere. concede propicius
familie tue; ut eo interueniente mereatur in se antiqui
hostis intatamenta superando extinguere. Per xpm
dominum nostrum. Amen.

The noble story to putte in remembrance
Of saynt Edmund, martyr, mayde & knyght
With his support my stile I wyl avaunce
ffirst to compile, aftur my kunnyng
His glorious lif, his birthe and his crownyng
And be discent, how that he that was so good
Was in sweden born, of the roial blood

In rethorik though that I haue no floure
Ner no coloures, his story tenlumyne
I dar not calle to Clio for socour
Nor to tho muses that been in nouhre nyne
But to this martir his grace tenclyne
To forthir my penne of that I wolde write
His glorious lif to translate and endite

For be sentence of prudent Carnotense
In Eutheticon where he doth specefie
Grace forthereth more than doth eloquence
Whiche of alle vertues hath the regalie
ffor Mercurie nothir Philosophie
To gidre knet and ioyned in mariage
Withoute grace may haue noon auantage

For grace hath power alle vertues to directe
Withouten whom auailith no prudence
ffor this princesse hath fredham to correcte
Al vicious thinges al slouthe al negligence
Which halt the reyne of wisdam and science
And but she gouerne of our lif the bridel
What euer we do we werke but in ydil

Withoute grace ech vertu is bareyn
Withoute grace force is but feblilesse
Withoute grace al wisdam is but veyn
Withoute grace may be no rihtwisnesse
ffredam bounte manhod nor gentilesse
Prowesse in armis nor sheltrous in bataile
Withoute grace what may al this availe

She set in ordre alle vertues be reson
Preserueth tunges from al froward langage
And she restreyneth thorugh hir hih renon
The cours of fortune for al hir fel outrage
And grace kan best sweten the passage
Of folk in labour which that dispeire
To reste eternall to make hem to repeire

Grace of the stronge double kan the strengthe
And she the feble kan supporte in his riht
And make a dwerf of a cubit lengthe
Venquysshe a geant for al his grete myht
Which callid is in euery mannys syht
Gouerneresse of vertues alle
Therfore to grace for helpe I wil now calle

And first this martir shal for me prouide
And of his mercy opne me the gate
To make grace forto be my guide
His holi lyf in ynglissh to translate
And to remembre the statly royal date
Whan I first gan on this translacion
It was the yeer by computacion

Whan syxte Henry in his estat royal
With his sceptre of yngland and of ffrance
Heeld at Bury the feste pryncipal
Of cristemesse with ful greet habundance
And aftur that list to haue plesance
As his consail gan for hym prouide
There in his place til hesterne forto abide

Whiche is an hous of his fundacion
Where his preestes synge ay for him and preie
Of ful hool herte and trewe affeccion
That god his noblesse in al vertu conueie
And graunte him wynne toforn or that he deie
A palme of conquest and whan that he shal fyne
To be regestred amongt the worthy nyne

Which at departyng in Bury from his place
Lyst of his noblesse and magnanymyte
And of his owyn special grace
Meuyd in hym silf of his benignyte
Of ther chapitle a brother forto be
Prayng his chapleyns occasion and matier
Ay to remembre on hym in ther prayer

For thei conceyue in ther opynyoun
Hooh the holy martir which restith in that place
Shal to the kyng be ful proteccioun
Ageyn alle enmyes be vertu and grace
And for his noblesse procure and purchace
fforto rassemble by tryumphal victory
To his fadir most notable of memory

Prayng atteynt that the kyng shal for his sake
Been to that church diffence and protectour
And into his handis al her quarel take
To been ther sheeld and ther supportour
Sithe he allone is ther total foundour
Them to releue ageyn al wordly shoures
Lyk as toforn did his progenitoures

And sithe the kyng / in his roial estat
List be devocioun / of his benyuolence
With the holy martir / to be confederat
As kyng with kyng / bothe of their excellence
ffor whiche the martir / be heuenly preemynence
To swte Herry / shal his grace dresse
To make hym floure / in tryumphal prowesse

The influence he / fro the heuene doun
Shal in knyhthod / make hym most marcial
Yiue hym with Arthour / noblesse and hih renoun
And with charlemayn / forto been egal
And he shal graunte hym / in especial
With seint Edward / to loue god and drede
And with seint Lowis / that was of his kynrede

In this mater / there is no more to seyn
Sauf to the kyng / forto do plesaunce
Thabbot William / his humble chapeleyn
Gaf me in charge / to do myn attendaunce
The noble story / to translate in substaunce
Out of the latyn / aftir my kunnyng
He in ful purpos / to yeue it to the kyng

And thouh I was bareyn of elloquence
Navyng no practik fresshley to endite
I took upon me vndur obedience
Aftir his biddyng me lowly forto qwite
But yit a foen or I gan to write
Vpon my knees / riht thus I gan to seie
To the holi martir and meekly forto preie

O precious charboncle / of martirs alle
O heuenly gemme / saphir of stablinesse
Thyn heuenly dewh of grace / let doun falle
In to my penne / enclosed with rudnesse
And blissid martir / my stile do so dresse
Vndur thi wenttis of proteccion
That I nat erre in my translacion

Richest rube / rubefied with blood
In thi passion / be ful meek suffraunce
Bounde to a tre / lowly whan thou stood
Of ardes sharp / suffrying ful gret penaunce
Stable as a wal / of herte in thi constaunce
Directe my stile / which haue vndirtake
In thi worsshepe / thi legende forto make

Lamettyst with peynes purpureat
Emeraud trewe / of chastite most cleene
Which nat withstandyng thi knyght high estat
ffor cristus feith / suffredist peynes keene
Wherfore of mercy / my dulnesse to susteene
Into my brest / sende a confortatiff
Of sum fair langage / tenbelisshe with thi liff

Send thou of grace / thi licour aureat
Which enlumynyth / these rethoriciens
To write of martirs / ther passious laureat
And causith also / these fressh musiciens
ffals lust auoided / of epicuriens
Of glorious seyntes / the tryumphes forto synge
That suffred peyne for crist in ther leuynge

Hold glorious martir / of Bury cheef patrou[n]
In Savoie born / of the blood roial
Conuere my mater / be my proteccio[u]n
Sithe in thi support / myn hope abidith al
Directe my penne / of that I write shal
ffor so thi fauour / fro me natt ne twynne
Vpon thi story / thus I wil begynne

In Sazonye whilom ther was a kyng
Callid Alkmond, of excellent noblesse
A manli prince, vertuous of leuyng
And ful habounde, of tresour and richesse
Notable in armys, ful renomed of prowesse
A semly persone, hardi and corageous
Mercurie in wisdam, lik mars victorious

Lyved as Artus, be vertuous prouidence
And circumspect, as famous Scipion
In kynght honour, of most excellence
Holde in his tyme, thorugh many a region
But nat withstandyng his famous high renon
He so demened his high noblesse in deede
Aboue al tresour, to loue god and dreede

In worldli honour, though he were fortunat
Set in a chaier, of kynght dignite
He koude knowe, in his roial estat
Aboue alle kynghts, god hath the souereynte
And aduertisid, in his most majeste
That sceptre or crownne may litil auaile, or nought
To hem that loue not god, in herte and thought

God makith kyngis / and god kan kast hem dŭ
Chastisith the proude / the meek he kan auaunce
Lyk ther merites / he yeueth hem ther guerdŏu
And hem aquyteth / aftir ther gouernaunce
This hadde Alkmond / ful weel in remembraunce
Which in his grettest / and most magnificence
To god disposid / to do most reuerence

For euery thyng that to god was dewe
Al obseruances / heuenly and deuyne
This worthi kyng / ful lowly wolde shewe
His roial crowhne / meekly to hym enclyne
Thus in two wise / his noblesse dide shyne
Toward the world / in knyghtly high prowesse
And toward god / in parfit holynesse

And of his noblesse / ferthere to declare
A wiif he hadde / the story berith witnesse
A worthi pryncesse / and callid was Gilbare
Which bothe excellid / in bounte and fairnesse
As Hester meek Judith in stabilnesse
And in beute lik Dido of Cartage
In wifly trouthe / void of al outrage

As lucrece she was of herte stable
In semlynesse resemblynge Bersabe
Sobre of hir port of wil nat variable
Lik marcia in wisly chastite
With al hir vertues passyng fair to se
Of compassion dide ay hir silf delite
In almesse dede, and poore folk to visite

Thus alkmundus with the queen Silvare
A feen of god chose it is no drede
As sumtyme was habraham and Sare
The holy patriark who so take hede
Of whos progenye blissid was the sede
Blissid ther stok, blissid ther roial blood
Which ther tyme bare frut that was so good

This kyng in herte hadde a devocioun
Petir and Poule in Rome to vesite
Shewid to hym be revelacioun
Wherof in soule he gretly than delite
And of affeccioun his wittes to aquite
Disposid hym to take that viage
And to parfourme his holi pilgrymage

Ryht fortunat he was in his passage
Reliques in rome devoutly vysytyng
With a widwe he took his herbertage
A parfit lady ful holy of leuyng
Which by miracle out of his brest stirryng
Sawh a cleer sonne with a ful heuenly lyht
That to foure parties shadde his beemys bryht

Wherupon she cauhte a fantasie
And in hir self than thoghtly ymagynyne
With a sperit fulfillid of prophecie
Sadly seide the sonne that I se shyne
Shewith in his stremys hostly and devyne
A pronostik as I conceyue in deede
Out of his brest a sonne shal out spreede

That shal enlumyne with his bemys cleer
The foure parties of the firmament
Shyne in vertu as phebus in his speer
Whan he his wayn hath from aurora sent
Voidyng alle cloudis with which the soil was blent
Makyng his stedis thorugh ther fery leemys
Glade thorison of many sondry reemys

For lik a sonne this worlds tenlumyne
From kyng Edmond a braunche shal out spreede
Which to al vertu his corage shal enclyne
As in his story heeraftur men shal reede
And in this mater ferthere to proceede
Of the holi womman he hath his leue take
And to Saxonie his viage he gan make

A**s solemply / there he was receyued
The contre thad / of his repeir a geyn
And aftir soone / Eluare hath conceyued
Thorugh goddis grace / that werketh neuer in veyn
And in that yeer / she bar a child certeyn
In Norenberghes / a cite of gret fame
Of hed prouided / Edmond was his name**

Eyhte hundrid yeer fourty and eek oon
Afftir cristis birthe by computacion
The same tyme so longe it was agoon
That this Edmond as maad is mencion
Was in Saxonie the noble region
Born of Alkbare by record of wrytyng
Sone to Alkmond the holi glorious kyng

He which Edmond bi grace of Crist Jhu
Day by day so as he grew in age
So he allwey encreced in vertu
Sobre of his chier void of al outrage
Demeur of port Angelik of visage
Most acceptable in every mannys siht
ffor of his presence glad was every wiht

Good frut ay cometh fro trees that be goode
ffrom fressh heed spryngges renne stremys cristallyne
In vertuous pastures holsom is the foode
ffro gentil blood procedith a trewe lyne
Taryge of trees thapplis determyne
So yong Edmond pleynly to declare
Shewed hoth he kam fro Alkmond and Arbare

His name Edmond / compossyd is of tweyne
That on party / seid of Blissidnesse
And the seconde / by vertu souereyne
Is seid also / of vertuous clennesse
And thus Edmundus pleynly to expresse
Of good a bove / lik as it was seene
Was bothe blissid / and of his lif most cleene

Fro thood / in vertu to bettre he dide encresse
By proporcion / of a good stature
ffor roial nature / koude neuer cesse
Of hir handwerk / to shewe the portrature
Louyd and desirid / of euery creature
ffor god gaff him / bi heuenly influence
Goute with wisdam / bewte with hih prudence

And thouh that he excellid in semlynesse
Was most heuenly / in chier and contenance
Yit was ther neuer / seyn vngentilesse
In his persone / nor in his gouernance
ffor of hih trouthe / and iust perseuerance
Afferme I dar / his lif who list discerne
Of alle goode thewes / he was liht and lanterne

Pryde in his persone hadde noon Interesse
Goodly of spech / to hih and lou3 de3ire
And though his birthe / was of hih noblesse
His port was coueied / with al humylite
Which of alle vertues / hath the souereynte
ffor wher meeknesse / bridle kan disdeyn
In hih estatis / there is noon errour seyn

Chast of his lif / bothe in deede and thou3t
Deuout to god ward / neuer out of charite
What euer he seide / his woord ne chau{n}gid he nou3t
Benygne of speche / to hih and lou3 de3ire
Disdeyned folk nou3t / in ther pouerte
But of nature / for al his hih renoun
Hadde on alle needy / roial compassioun

For vertu that by / take in tendre a3e
Where grace graueth / the deepe impressiou{n}
It wilnat voide / by no foreyn outra3e
But more encrece / by longe successiou{n}
Loue take in youthe / hath this condicious
In gentil hertis / for tenduren euere
By neshe encres / and neuer to disseuere

Yong of yeeris, old of discrecion
Flouryng in age, fructuous of sadnesse
His sensualite, ay soget to reson
And of his counsail, discrecion was maistresse
Foure cardynal sustre, fforce and rihtwisnesse
Weied alle his werkis by prudence in ballance
A passious wiide, in his attemperance

Though he was fair as Alcibiades
And with Dauid hadde grace vnto his mekenesse
ffor alle these vertues in his roial encres
He was deuoid of surquedie and pride
Vices alle in him were set a side
And yf he shal be shortly comprehendid
In him was no thyng forto be amendid

He whom that god list of his grace calle
To his seruise thoruh hih perfeccion
He wil fro vertu nat suffre him forto falle
But singulerly in his prouision
Stablysshe ther corages and ther profession
Hool in his feith, such grace he doth hem sende
So to preserue, onto his lyues eende

And to procede ferthere in this mater
Yf ye list aduertise in your mynde
An exciplaure and a merour cler
In this story ye shal noCh seen and fynde
ffor yong Edmond listnuit be behynde
With othre martirs most parfit chose and good
ffor cristis feith forto shede his blood

And the processe pleynly to declare
Of Estyngtland how he was maad kyng
To as I kan in soth I wil nat spare
But heer in ordre rehersse by Wrytyng
ffollhyng myn auctours in every maner thyng
As in substance Vpon the lettre in deede
To do plesance to them that shal it reede

How he was sacryd kyng
of Estyngtland and by
What title he kam to the
Crowne

The same tyme remembrid heer toforn
As ye han herd, the processe by reedyng
Whan seynt Edmond was in Saxonie born
In Estyngland, reyned a worthy knyht
A manly man, and vertuous of levyng
Weel gouerned, and of notable fame
And as I fynde, Offa was his name

Longe in that rewm his lif he dide leede
In his estat, with ful gret worthynesse
But for he hadde noon heir to succeede
He kauhte in herte a maner hevynesse
Which to refourme devoutly and redresse
Ther kam a conceit in to his wittes
Onto holy lond to make a pilgrymage

Which for taccomplisshe he made his purveyance
List no lenjtere delaie it nor respite
His rewm first in good governance
Thouhte by the way his cosyn to visite
And forth he goth pleynly to endite
On his viage with a gret meyne
Toward Savoye and passid is the see

And ther he was receyued lik a kyng
Of Alkmundus his oebyn cosyn dere
And alle estatis in Savoye abidyng
Assemblid theren forto make him chiere
And specially his nevew most entiere
Blissid Edmond with toial attendance
Was ay awaitynt him to do plesance

He neuer parted out of his presence
To him he hadde so gret affeccion
Which that kyng Offa in his aduertence
Ful weel considered of wysdam and reson
Seyng in vertu his disposicion
Dempte him ful able as by liklynesse
For tatteyne to vertuous hih noblesse

Of face and look he was so amyable
Best accepted in euery mannys siht
Demene of port of his chier most stable
On his bealoncle awaitynt day and nyht
Al this considered thouhte as it was ryht
Hou he muste of reson and nature
Loue Edmond best aboue ech creature

First in his conceit he gan to takyn heed
To his neuew/how moch that he was boude
Thouhte ageynward/in blood and nyh kynreed
How riht requyrith/where gentilesse is foude
Of kyndly mevyng/it must ageyn reboude
To him where first/the gentilesse was seyn
Loute for loute/for loue shewe loue ageyn

Which kyng Offa gan wisly aduertise
Of his neuew/seyinge the diligence
The grete attendance/thabaytyng the seruise
The humble port/thabood in his presence
Alle these thyngis/kyngly to recompense
Thouhte he was boude/to hym al his liff
Hym to guerdone with sum prerogatiff

Thus euery thyng/that was necessarye
Wisly ordeyned/toward his passage
This worthy Offa list no lengere tarye
Than he were redy/to doon his pilgrymage
Except a sparkle/abood in his corage
Of hih feruence/toward his neuew dere
And to hym seide/riht thus as ye shal here

First in his armys he than hym to embrace
And seide Edmond my neuew most entier
My wil is this / or I parte fro this place
And swill also / that alle men it heere
Because thow hast maad me so good cheere
What euer falle of myn ageyn komyng
Or I departe receyue of me this ryng

And gentil neuew / in especiall
I the accepte for my sone in deede
Vnder most trewe affeccion paternall
Aforn alle othre of my kynreede
Of riht hool herte / that thow shalt succede
The croune tenherite and regne after my day
Yif it so falle / I deye be the wey

With salt teerys, dystyllyng on his face
At his departyng, of fadirly feruence
Eft ageyn Edmond he gan enbrace
His cosyn Alkmund, beyng in presence
Which every thyng, markid in sentence
That kyng Offa outher dede or saide
Unto his sone, and smylyng this he saide

Osmond sone, hastow me forsake
And list of me nomore to taken heed
And of affection a newe fadir take
Which art so nyh born, of his kynreed
And sithe it likith, to his goodlyheed
To take the so, and forto be thy guyde
As for his sone, lat hym for the provyde

Aftir this langage, Offa took a ryng
Which was to hym most special and entiere
With which he was, afforn ysacred kyng
By an holy bysshop, the story doth us lere
And onto Edmond he seide in this manere
Gentil nevew, this ryng which that thow dost se
Shal been a token, atwyxe the and me

What our or tyme, that I this ryng the sende
Receyue it goodly, for an entier sygne
Which in effect shal be for a good eende
And for sum cause of memorye digne
Which for taccomplysshe, be gracious and benygne
Touchyng my sonde, take good heed therto
Withoute delay, anoon that it be do

Alle the statis of Saxonye were present
At the departyng, of these kyngis tweyne
Conueyeng Offa alle of on assent
With that noblesse which thei dede ordeyne
At leue takyng, thei felte a manier peyne
But it was seid, sithe ho many a yeer
That freendis alwey, may not been in feer

Ossa goth forth, and Alkmund stille a bood
Riht weel beseyn, and with a fayr meyne
And ful devoutly on his way he rood
Toward the parties of the grete se
At bood the passage, ye grete no mor me
ffor be the story I can not deuise
Where he shippid, at Gene, or at Venyse

Of his passage by that se so large
Nor by what costis his galey dide dryue
It is no parcell pleynly of my charge
Thurhouth tounes cleerly to descryue
Nor wher ther speed was, outher slouh or blyue
It is a thyng which I nat vndirtook
Be cause it is nat rehersid in my book

I hadde neuer rad afforn nor seyn
Of ffranceys Petrak / the Cosmagraffie
Where he descryueth / ful openly and pleyn
The straunge contres / toward that partie
And how the maistrys / shal ther Galeys guye
Of old expert / touchyng ther loodmanmage
Which to declare / I haue no cleer langage

But whan he had accomplysshyd his iourne
At the holy Sepulcre / doon his deuocioun
And certeyn daies / abide in that contre
In his praieres / and special orisons
ffulfillid his vowes / maad his oblacions
Glad in his herte / that he the place hath seyn
His vessell reedy / gan shape hym hoom ageyn

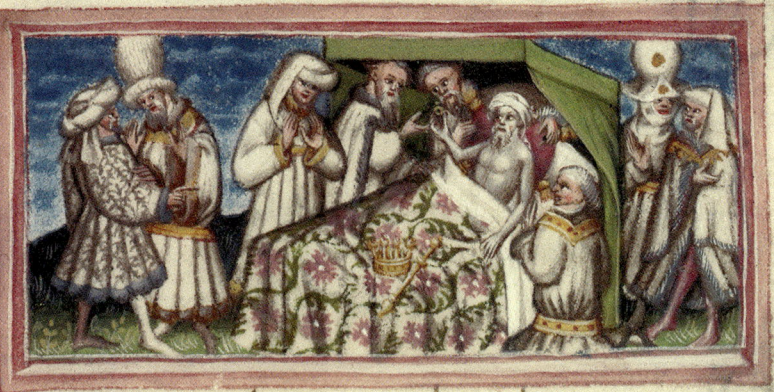

And as the story / cleerly doth expresse
In his repair / this holy blyssid kyng
At port Seyntgeorge / fil in gret seeknesse
And ther a while / vpon his bed lyggyng
fful weel conceyued / in his languysshyng
Be the encressyng / of his maladie
That he muste die / there was no remedie

And ful deuoutly / of humble and meek entent
He made him redy / by confessiovn
Thanne receyued / the holy sacrament
Gan to declare / his hertis mocioun
All his meyne / stondyng eviroun
To-forn them alle / in open audience
And first of alle / tolde hem this sentence

Syrs quod he I charge yow in deede
And yow coniure, of conscience to se
Touchyng my kyngdham, who that shal succede
T'auoide alway, al ambiguyte
My laste will takith heed that it so be
Ye this in soth, seith so at your repeyr
My cosyns sone, shal reigne and be myn heyr

Hath, berth my neuew, this tokne and this ryng
After the promys maad, whan that I wente
In al haste possible, that he be crownyd kyng
Besechyng yow, in al my beste entente
Withoute delay, this massage to presente
Aftir my deth, and looke ye nat varye
To my desir, forto been contrarye

Let been amonge yow, no contencion
In this matier, nor no variance
But that ye putte him in cleer pocession
Of Estynytland, to haue the gouernance
This is my will, this is myn ordynance
And my desir, looke it be do soone
ffor sondry vertues I se in his persone

I wot

But both he hath disposicioun
Unto al vertu as semeth unto me
And god hath sent him of grace that foyson
Semlynesse wisdam and beaute
Loue and that fauour of hih and lowh degree
Which in o persone to rekne be riht fayr
Therfore at o woord I wil he be myn hayr

And whan his meyne which knelid hym beforn
Had herd the wil and sentence of the kyng
With that assurance they were bounde and sworn
It for taccomplisshe in every maner thyng
And whan he hadde delyuered hem the ryng
Of this lyff heer makyng a blysful eende
To god his mercy his soule he dide sende

Han his meyne, with al ther besy cure
As they best koude, in straunge fer contre
Gan ordeyne for his sepulture
And buryed hym with gret solempnite
Which accomplisshid, they taken han the se
By goddis grace, makyng no dellaies
Into Saronie they kam in felbe daies

To kyng Alkmond, ther message first thei tolde
Of kyng Offa and of his fair eendyng
And he gan weepe, as he to water wolde
And to yonge Edmond, they presente vp the ryng
And hym besouhte, þat maner constreynyng
In goodly haste, for deyne his passage
Toward Estyngland, taccepte his heritage

His fadir Alkmond trist in compleynyng
Kepte his chambre where his clothis blake
ffrom al peple his persone absentyng
Til be processe his sorwe gan aslake
Than in his paleis he gan a counseil make
Of alle his lordis of which as were most wys
In this matier to heren there avys

Wher that his sone grene and tendir of age
By ther discrecion and noble providence
Shal forth procede to take his heritage
Toward Estynglond bauys of the sentence
ffor he was loth to leven his presence
Sithe al his gore and worthy suffisance
A hood in Edmond and his herthy plesance

And with o vois they concluse everychon
ffynally this matier to termyne
To Estynglond that Edmund sholde gon
Ther to be crowned next born off that lyne
ffor they dempte be grace which is dyvyne
And off ther counsail hool and undevyded
That he off thos was therto provyded

Lern whos wil may be no resistence
Nor no consail which that may auaile
ffor god preferreth thorugh his magnyficence
Alle tho in vertu which that may preuayle
Whos disposicion most vnkouth off entayle
Aforn ordeyneth þe merueillous werkynges
The palme off prynces and crollynyng eek off kynges

Alkmund was heuy off cheer and contenance
That Edmund sholde departe out off his sith
With wepyng eyen, hauyng remembrance
Off thilke woman that sawh a sonne bryht
Shyne on his brest that haff so cleer a lyht
In rome cite, and kauhte a fantesie
How thilke sonne dide Edmund sighnefie

Which was a tokne that he sholde in this lyff
Shyne lik a sonne by excellent cleernesse
And off foure vertues han a prerogatiff
Ffirst off Prudence, off fforce and Ryhtwisnesse
Hys batemperance in his chast clennesse
That he be sutnes which were in hym begonne
Sholde in al vertu shyne lik an heuenly sonne

These thynges peised, and weied in his thouht
And in him sylff enspired off reson
By goddis wil how al this thyng was wrouht
And off hih wisdam and discrecion
He condescendid to the peticion
Off thembassiat dewly as him ouhte
Which the massageris from kyng offa brouhte

First twenty knyhtes he ches out off his rewm
That wern in wysdam, and knyhthod most notable
And other twenty, that fro Iherusalem
Kam with kyng Offa, famous and honurable
And among alle, a knyht off port most stable
Assynned was, the story is ffull kouth
ffor to gouerne Edmund in his youth

He hadde off old famous experience
Bothe off armys, and off gentilesse
Al his aport demened with prudence
Sadnesse in tyme, in tyme also gladnesse
With entrechaungyngis off merthe and sobirnesse
Affter the sesons requered off euery thyng
A man ful able to been a bovte a kyng

He hadde eek clerkis ful cicumspect and wise
Guynes talbarte vpon his doctryne
Chose chapeleyns erly for tarise
To do seruyse which that is dyuyne
And alle his sodieres pleynly to termyne
Sodieres and yomen that sholde with him goon
Eksamynd for vertu ches hem everychoon

And affter this as he that was ful wys
Ordeyne than ful royal apparayle
For yonge Edmund be dillygent avys
Stuffed his shippis with meyne and vitayle
And whan they weern redy for to sayle
This chose off god ful meekly doun knelyng
Off ffader and mooder axeth the blessyng

It nedeth nat / to wryten or reherse
The wofull sobbynges / the sythes to declare
Nor the heuynesses / that than the hertis perse
Off al that land / whan Edmund sholde fare
The pitous wepynges / off Alkmund and Gisbare
How they in terys / than hem sylven drowne
Nor off this Alkeen / how ofte she dide swowne

This noble pryncesse / koude hir nat restreyne
Whan that she sawh / hir sone take his leue
To sobbe and weepe / and pitously compleyne
It was no wonder / though it dide hym greue
ffor tendre moodres / ther loue kan wel preue
Herth tokenys to shewe / out / kan not spare
Thorwh mortal constreynt / rerd vpon Sylvare

Whan she hir sone / than kyssen and enbrace
And in hir armys / moderly hym streyne
With salt terys / bedewed al hir face
So bitter was the partyng / off them tweyne
And in especial / most she felte peyne
Whan she sawh Edmund / entren in to se
She koude nat stynte / to wepyn off pite

Off al that day she list nat for to pleye
Nor no man kowde make hir glad nor light
ffor whan the shyppis gan saile vpon the weye
She stood sty stylle and affter cast hir siht
So weel as moodres loue ther kan no wiht
And whan Sylvare hadde longe mourned
Conueyed in armys hoom she is retourned

Expert the shypmen / off ther loodmanage
Knowyng the costis / off ech sond
And Eolus fortuned / ther passage
And God by grace / heeld ouer them his hond
Conueied ther shyp / toward Estlond
And at a place / pleynly to descryue
Callyd Maydenburuth / in haste they dide aryue

Thoruh goddis myht whan thei the lond han kauht
This holi Edmond of hool affeccion
ffro ther arryuaile almost a bowe drauht
He ful deuouutly gan to knele doun
And preied god first in his orison
That his comyng were to him acceptable
And to al the land welful and profitable

And in tokne that god herde his praier
Vpon the soil sondy hard and drie
Ther sprout bi myracle fyue wellis cler
That been of vertu helthe and remedie
Ageyn ful many straunge malladie
Thus list the lord of his eternal myht
ffirst at his londyng magnefie his knyht

Alle the feeldis sowyn rownd aboute
And lond arable a ful large space
Gan there tencrece of trouthe this no doute
More than it dide in any othir place
And al thencres kam of goddis grace
ffor in such caas may been noon obstacle
Whan for his seynt god werketh bi myracle

And be side the wellis as I fynde
At his comyng she bilt a roial toun
Which stant ther yit for a maner mynde
ffor his arryuaile into this regioun
Which is this day callid Hunstantston
And betokneth who so looke a right
In latyn tonge Swetnesse and met nyght

For this name componyd is of tweyne
ffirst of Hony which hath gret swetnesse
The tother party pleynly forto seyne
Ys seid of stonys which han gret hardnesse
And thus this toun pleynly to expresse
Of Ston and Hony took ther proprte
Of folk that first dwellid in that cite

For they were humble of maneres and tretable
Pesible of port and of condicious
And at a proef manly and dissensable
And for tassaile lik hardy champions
In pes lik lambes in werre lik leons
And in this wise this manly peple wroughte
Which fro Saxonye seynt Edmond broughte

A ND ther he heeld his houshold wth a yeer
And thanne remeued to Athelborgh the toū
And there I fynde he lerned his saulteer
And in this while of fals collusioū
Ennyes were entred into this regioū
Which falsly hadde of ther malis contryued
ffrom his kyngdham Edmond to haue depryued

Thei caste of fforce rather than of right
To haue put hym from his heritage
But a for god trouthe passith myht
Ne gifte ne blood hauyng auantage
And though so were that he was yong of age
God wolde his title promoten in certeyn
Maugre alle tho that truede ther ageyn

ffor whan

For whan Humbertus the bysshop Elmanense
Knew the purpos of the fals werkyng
Made alle the lordes thorugh his hih prudence
Of thilke kyngisham to come at his callyng
And of kyng Offa shewed hem the ryng
Whos laste wil he dede to them expresse
His stward present that therof bar witnesse

Twenti knyhtis that were at his endyng
The trouthe holy of this mater
Thus by grace ther was no mor taryeng
The lordis first with al the peeple i feer
Jsful loude cried that all myhte hier
That of kyng Offa be gifte and be kynreede
Edmond was heir iustly to succeede

And of assent heeron a day they sette
List no while prolonge it nor delaie
But alle attones att Withburgh hym sette
In the beste wise they koude hem silf araie
Wherof his enemyes wreth than dismaie
But alle such enemyes to hyndryn han no myht
Where bi grace god list to forthre a ryht

Gret noübre of lordes and worthy knyhtis sadde
Bothe of Gascoyne and this region
Fful ryaly this yonge prynce ladde
Toward Suffolke as maad is mencion
And hym conueied to the roial toü
Callid Bures who so list to lere
Where he was crowned anoon as ye shal heere

Hauf whit and blak y haue no mo colowres
Fforto descryue his coronacion
In Tullius gardeyn y fadrid neuer flowres
Nor neuer slepte vpon Citheron
Nor at the welle drank of Elycon
Nor of Calliope no fauour fond attall
To telle or write a feste so royall

I haue therto no kunnyng, nor insiht
fforto reherse so excellent a thyng
ffor he receyued that day by goddis myht
A crowne a sceptre a swerd eek and a ryng
And by humbertus he was enoynted kyng
fful solempnely the cronycle ye may see
The day of cristis hih Natyuyte

The riche crowne was set on his hed
To reule the peeple, thorugh his hih noblesse
And heeld the swerd, to keepe al vndir dreed
That dide wrong the peeple to oppresse
The Sceptre of pees the kyng of ryhtwisnesse
ffor pees and riht with mercy meynt among
Conserue a kyng in his estat most strong

This thyng accomplisshid by accomptes cleer
ffro the tyme of thyncarnacion
Eihte hundryd wyntir fifty and seue yeer
Whan blissid Edmond thorugh his hih renon
Was crowned at Suevys kyng of this region
Which that tyme most gracious of vysage
Was ful compleet fiftene yeer of age

This chapitle declareth the roial
gouernance of seynt Edmond
aftir he was crowned kyng of
Estyngland.

This hih feste ful famous of renoun
ffully accomplisshid with every circustance
On al that longith tacoronacioun
That blyssid Edmond by goddis ordynaunce
Hadde of Estynglande hool the gouernance
Thogh most beyng euer his mynde
ffirst for his reem thus he than prouyde

Lawes he sette of trouthe and equite
Them establysshid upon ryhtwisnesse
ffirst so disposynyt his royal mayeste
Then sceptre and swerd tattempre his noblesse
That ther were fonde in nouther noon excesse
But with the Sceptre conserue his peeple in pees
Punysshe with the swerd folk that were rekles

ffor as a sceptre is smothe long and round
The hier part of gold and stonys ynde
So semblably this noble kyng Edmond
Was meek of maneres and vertuous as I fynde
Up to thoward hadde most his mynde
Mercy preferryng examyned euery dede
Delayed rygour lystnat of haste procede

In his on hand the sceptre of pees he heeld
Cherisshyng his peeple in reste and quyete
And wher that he espied or beheeld
Ryot or trouble of folk that were vnmeete
Of manly prudence in his royal seete
Anoon he took his swerd of rihtwisnesse
Of fals rauyne alle surfetis to redresse

And so of clerkys/ as Discrecion
Ys named moodir/ of vertues alle
With hir douhtren/ prouydence and reson
Fikst to sustene/ she kowde natt nor falle
So was she besy/ the tresour that men calle
Rem publicam/ to meuen and amende
In pees/ tallmente tt in werre tt to diffende

He kowde the reynes/ coarten and restreyne
Of such as lyued/ by fals robberye
Al ydul folk that wolde also disdeyne
In vertuous labour/ ther bodies to applie
Chastise truantis/ for ther losengrye
Denly cheryshe/ as it is specefied
For comon profit/ them that were occupied

In foure thyngis he dide his besynesse
Ffirst sette his study/ bi ful gret dullygence
With hool herte/ and vertuous hih prowesse
Doon first to god/ dwe reuerence
Cheryshe his prynces/ in ther magnificence
Gouerne his knyhtis/ in martial dyscyplyne
Tauht by vigecius famous in that doctryne

First blyssid Edmond / of noble policie
Heeld up the church / of hih perfection
ffro them avoided / al maner symonye
Bothe ypocrisie / and symylacion
Gaff no beneficees / but for devocion
But ches out heerdis / most contemplatyff
To reule his peeple / for ther parfit liff

His roial Juges / that shulde his doomys speede
Such as excellid / in kunnyng and prudence
That were nat corrupt / with favour loue nor dreede
And hadde to giftes / no maner aduertence
Groundid in lawe / and on good conscience
Them he ches out / by whos auysementis
Were execut hooly his Iuggementis

His noble lawes / that tyme were gouernyd
Withoute oppression / of any meyntenance
That lyht of trouthe / cleerly was discernyd
And nat eclipsid / be power nor puissance
ffor meede tho daies / peysed nat in ballance
Nor fals forsweryng / with favour was not meynt
Nor for vntrouthe / Iurours were not atteynt

Marchandise / sold by no gyle
The symple biggere / vntrewly to deceyue
Thartificer / knew no maner wile
Nowther in vttryng / nor inward to receyue
What fraude mente / men koude nat tho conceyue
The laborer / neded no staff to borwe
ffor his salarie / aboodnat til the morwe

Thus first of prynces / the notable excellence
And of the cherch / the preued perfeccion
And of the Iuges / thairyse prouydence
And of knyghthod / the martial hih renon
And of marchantis / the hih discrecion
With al the residue / in oon ymage knet
Wher by kyng Edmund / in ther deW ordre set

Of this ymage / prynces stood as hed
With ther two eyen / of prudence and reson
To ther sottetis / forto takyn heed
That thei nat erre / by no devysion
Eek that the eeris / haue inclynacion
That outher party / his quarell may expresse
Be good leiser / or ther here domys dresse

This moral ymage / to conserue and diffende
The kyng ordeyned / of royal polycye
That worthy knyhtis / pleynly to comprehende
Sholde of the armys / the party occupie
fforto supporte it / thorwh ther chyualrie
To keepe maidens / and widwes / from outrage
And saue the chirche / from myschef and damage

This cristene prynce / for a prerogatyff
Disposed a soule / to quyke this ymage
fforto preserue folk / contemplatyff
Sobre of ther leuyng / demeur and sad of age
Expert in kunnyng / benygne of ther langage
Yif ther office / be example / and by doctryne
With liht of vertu his peeple tenlumyne

With feet and leggys / this ymage to supporte
To contynue bi lengthe / of many yeeris
This prynce ordeyned / his story kan reporte
The plouh in cheeff / with othir laboreris
As dyuers trauailes / which been particuleris
ffor but yif labour / holde the plouh on honde
In prosperite / no lond ne myhte stonde

Thus euery membre / set in ordre dewe
Cause was noon / among hem to compleyne
ffor ech of hem / his office dide shewe
The hed lisnat / at the foot disdeyne
Ther loue was oon / departed not on tweyne
Ech thyng bi grace / so deuly was conueied
Hed of the membris / was not disobeied

And as the ruby / kyng of stonys alle
Reioiseth ther presence / with his naturel liht
So kyng Edmond / in his roial stalle
With sceptre and crowne / sat lik an heuenly knyht
To hih and lowh / most agreable of syht
This woord rehersid / of euery creature
Longe mote he leue / longe mote the kyng endure

And as myn auctour his persone doth descryue
He was be craft so fourmyd of nature
A bettur compact was ther noon a lyue
Nor proporcyonnyd of fetures nor stature
Most lik a knyght labour to endure
And euery man only bi goddis grace
Loued hym of herte that loked on his face

In his estat most goodly and benygne
Heuenly of cher of counseil prouydent
Hadde in his persone many blissid signe
Whan tyme requyrid knyghtly pacient
And ay to godward hool was his entent
And al his port in ordre to termyne
Was to al vertu a scole and a doctryne

In his doomys most rightful & most tredle
Best auysid in iuggement yeuyng
Stable of his heste loued no chaunges newe
Koude weel abyde natt hasty in werkyng
And passendly discreet in comandyng
In his langage natt boistous nor contrarie
But with sad cher benygne and debonaire

Most temperat he was of his dieete
Large in yevyng / to folkes vertuous
To feyrenesse most mansuet and meete
In prosperite / meek / and natt pompous
But in aduersite / of mercy most famous
His hand mynystre / pleynly as I reede
Opne his cofres / for almesse deede

To alle religious / protectour and support
To heretikes / a yerde most mortal
Lollardis that tyme fond in hym no confort
To holichirche / he was so strong a wal
Hated fals dottryn / in especial
And disdeyned / of kyngly excellence
To alle fals tonges / to yeuen audience

To his hihnesse it was abhomynable
ffeynyd lesynges and adulacion
Rankrid mouthes and lippis detestable
And al envyous supplantacion
Hadde in his siht no sympectacion
Double corages nor sowders of discord
With his noblesse myht haue noon accord

And as myn auctour makith rehersaile
His hih prowesse puttynh in memorye
In trouthes quarel komynh to bataile
A sheeld of knyhthod of worthynesse the storye
Callid in armes a swerd of hih victorye
ffor in his brest he bar to his encres
Of magnanymyte the herte of Hercules

Prudence in armys to make a feeld and sette
Hadde with Nestor manly avysynesse
Knyhtly cherid his foomen whan he mette
With Tideus he hadde eek hardynesse
Eek at assailes passynh delyuernesse
And though he hadde bothe hardynesse and myht
He neuer took feeld but on a ground of ryht

What euer he wan, of ffredam and bountte
To parte it forth, he was most liberal
In his giftes there was no skarsete
ffor lougthe delaies he liste noon make attal
ffor of such giftes that callid been roial
men seyn with prynces who that hath to doone
A gifte is doublid whan it is youe soone

This prynce, among of natural gentilesse
Wolde for disport, his story doth devyse
Hawke and hunte, tauoiden ydilnesse
Use honest games, in many sondry wise
And lik a knyht, to haue exercise
With martial pleies, in youthe hauyn a guyde
Knyhtly to teche hym, for pees to Juste and ryde

And as it sat, to his roial estatt
Dyuers tymes, he armyd wolde be
To renne a pees, Wondir fortunat
Therin most ethrous and therwithal parde
Best demened, that men koude owher se
ffor god bi grace, maad hym so entier
That he was able, alle vertues to leer

This worthy prynce, famous in al vertu
Old of prudence, of yeris yong and greene
Chose and ordeyned, of our lord Jhu
Tencrece in goodnesse, of entent most cleene
ffor in his court, as it was weel seene
As his master in youthe, dide hym teche
Ther was noon oth, nor dishonest speche

ffirst in

First in the moelbe / whan he dide aryse
With his knyhtis / he was anoon conueied
To his oratorie / to heren his seruise
Al holy thyng / of him was so obeied
Cloos in his herte / ech uertu was y keied
Thus toward heuene he was contemplatiff
Toward the world / a good knyht of his liff

And of his houshold / stywarD was plente
Glad suffysance was his tresorer
And contvollour was lyberalite
And trewe rekenere / was callid his cofrer
And humble compassion / was his almener
Marchal of halle / good cher with gentilesse
And clerk of kechyn / was feithful rydynesse

There was no surfet / of no ryot late
Sobirnesse kepte his wach / at eue
Heyn poore folk / shet was not his gate
His wardrope open / alle needy to releue
Such roial mercy dide his herte meue
To clothe the nakid / and the hungry feede
And sente his almesse / to folk that lay bedreede

Who can or may, keepe cloos or hide
A cleer lanterne, whan that it is lyht
On a chaundelabre, whan it doth abide
Or of the sonne, diffface the bemys bryht
Or who koude hyndre, thoowis owne knyht
This holy Edmond, this cristes owne man
To many a kyng him, but that his fame ran

Of his nobleffe, that was the repoert
In Estyngland, how ther was a kyng
Of whom the renon, by many a strauhge poet
Was rad and fange, his vertues rehersyng
His gouernance, his knyhtly demenyng
Which cesid natt, for tyme it was be ronne
Til into Denmark, the noble fame is ronne

Which was occasion, of ful gret hatreed
Of such as hadde, at his nobleffe enuye
Prowesse of knyhthod, where euer it doth proceed
And hih repoert, of famous cheualrie
Is hyndred is ful ofte, on sum partie
Of them that lift falsly, therat disdeyne
Whan to such nobleffe, them silf may not atteyne

Now cese a while I wil in this matere
And in maner make a digression
Lyk as myn auctour doth me pleynly lere
fforto reherse the firste occasion
How danys kam into this region
Aftir reherse the title be wrytyng
Of the martirdam of this worthy kyng

Explicit liber primus Incipit secundus

Somtyme in Denmark ther was a paynym kyng
As I fynde Lothbrocus was his name
Which hym delited in hawkyng and huntyng
And to disporte him in such maner game
And for thencres of his roial fame
Whan he to Mars had doon his obseruance
To serue Diane was set al his plesance

This Lothbrocus hadde sones tweyne
Wonder despitous and of gret crueltee
Hynguar and Ubba which that dide here peyne
To stuffe ther shyppis with gret meyne
Lyk as piratis to robbe upon the se
And so lik men of ther cursse wood
Reioised hem euere to slen and shede blood

What euer they wan outher bi force or myht
It was to hem no maner difference
ffor whethir ther getyng kam by wrong or riht
They took ther title of wilful violence
And as they sat onys in the presence
Of Lothbrocus ther fadir that was kyng
They than boste and seide in auauntyng

Ys ther any lewyng / now these dayes
Kyng or prynce / so myhti of puissance
On any regiun / knowen at alle assaies
On londe and water / that hath gouernance
Which rassemblith / or is lik in assurance
To vs in manhod / yf it be declaryd
Which to our noblesse / of riht may be comparyd

ffor there is noon / afforn vs dar abide
Be title of swerd / alway we preuaile
To spoile be force / alle them that go or ride
Take alle vessellis / that in the se do saile
Stuf of marchantis / we proudly kan assaile
Takyng noon heed / whethir it be ryht or wrong
ffor ther be any / on erthe / now so strong

Whan Lothbrocus / had herd hem seid a while
Such bostful wordes / presumptuous of langwage
With noon on hem / of scorn he gan to smyle
Bad hem stynte / and cese of ther outrage
Seide / there was oon / yong and tendir of age
Which passed hem / in worthynesse as ferre
As doth the sonne / a verray litil sterre

In Estynyland, there reyneth now a kyng
Whos hih renon alle folkes do comende
Of whom the noblesse, by report of seyeng
On every part his bemys doth extende
Lat be your bost, his prowesse doth transcende
All your emprises, as hih as doth the moone
A cloudy skie, that shal vanysshe soone

With his manhod, he holden is rihtwis
And with his knyhthod, he hath gret providence
Of gouernance, he hath a souereyn pris
Thouh he be large, he doth no violence
And thus his famous roial excellence
I dar reherse, as men reporten alle
Doth your audautynyt and al your bost appalle

Thus hath the heuene disposid and his fate
That he in vertu hath no tyme lorn
And thouh so be, he was but late
As men recorde, in Capornie born
Spent weel his youthe, as I you tolde aforn
Sit now crownyd on a kynges state
Where ye no name han, sauf of fals pillage

Rehersith sum thyng, in especial
Which to your worshepe, may rebounde atteyn
Yif euer ye dide, any thyng egal
On londe or watir, that was knowe or seyn
Lyk the merites, preued in certeyn
Of kyng Edmond, which with sceptre in honde
But yong of yeris, gouerneth Estynglonde

With such rebukes, whan Lothbrok had hem blamyd
In ther hertis, it causid gret enuye
And of them silff, were verraily ashamyd
That the kyng Edmond, lift so magnefie
Made an a vow, of fals conspiracie
Yif thei myhte, fynde oportunyte
On his noblesse, thei wolde auengyd be

Thus euer hath been, a meruielous difference
Twen liht of uertu, and vecious derknesse
Twen perfeccion, and raueynous violence
Atwen fals pillage, and knyhtly hy prowesse
Enuye alwey, is contrary to goodnesse
And thus for uertu, to speke in wordes pleyne
Inguar and Hubba, at Edmond han disdeyne

And in this menewhyle/ it fil vpon a day
Of fantasie/ that cam onto his mynde
He wolde disporte him/ to take his hauk and play
This said Lothbrook/ and leue his men behynde
And at a ryuer/ it fil thus as I fynde
Because that he was allone at large
Anoon he entred in a litil barge

And in that vessel/ whil he kept hym cloos
Cool be hym silff/ that no man myght hym se
Al vnwarly/ a sodeyn wynd a roos
And drof his barge/ into the salt see
And by our occian/ daies too or thre
fforDreuen he was/ by fatal auenture
Among the wawes and koude no land recure

Diuers cuntrees he passid of many a sond
With sondry tempestis forpossid to and fro
Tyl be fortune he was cast upon the lond
Ffer up in Northfolke the story tellith so
Beside a village callid Redam tho
Men of the contre for an vnkouth thyng
Hym and his hauk presented to the kyng

Ryht merueilous and riht a straunge caas
A kyng to come fro so fer contre
And no man koude espie what he was
In his aport he kepte him so secre
Thyng that god wyl it must needis be
To muse theron the labour were in veyn
Or to dispute or argue ther ageyn

Whan Lothbrocus was to kyng Edmond brouht
The kyng comandid of roial gentilesse
To al his houshold that he failed nouht
Of that myhte ese hym in his heuynesse
Or reconforte hym in his vnkouth distresse
Euer of custum charnyng his officeres
Al humanite shewen to strauñgeres

Thoruh al his court this was the vsance
That no man shulde in no maner wise
To no strauñger do no displesance
But them cherysshe as thei best kan deuyse
Which of custum was kept for an enprise
In al his paleis to pilgrym and strauñger
With hool attendance that ech man make cheer

This said Lothbrok was weel ronne in age
Riht gentilmanly in al his demenyng
Was disposid of old in his corage
Specially to haukyng and huntyng
To whom ther was assigned by the kyng
Don that was maystur of his huntis alle
And as I fynde Beriñ men dide him calle

This lothbrocus considered every thyng
Though he were a paynym in his lyue
Tokyns notable / which he sauh in the kyng
Of his prowesse / and knyhtly discyplyne
And how he was / a merour of doctryne
And his houshold / was liht and lanterne
To alle vertuous / how thei shal hem gouerne

ffor which lothbrocus lowly as him ouhte
Requered the kyng / for him to prouide
with hool herte / of grace he him besouhte
In his houshold / that he myhte abide
Doon him seruise / bothe to gon and ride
ffor as him semyte / it was in his auys
A mong housholdis / an heuenly paradys

To whos request / the kyng is condescendid
And most goodly / than him reconforte
Gaf him licence / and nat be reprehendid
with seyn his huntis / to pleye him and disporte
And whan him list / to court ageyn resorte
And grauntid him / withoute daunger
To gon on haukyng / by euery fressh ryuer

And though Lothbrocus were of hih estat
In his contre, and of gret excellence
Yit in such game, he was most fortunat
And therof hadde famous experience
Thorugh whos besy waker dilligence
His hauk and he took foules many fold
Ech day them brouhte hoom to the houshold

Al watirfoul, and foul upon the lond
Wher he fond plente, in any maner place
Ther myht noon escape from his hond
And beestis wilde, ful weel he koude enchace
And thus he stood weel in the kynges grace
Eek al the houshold, than him murthesie
Sauf Bern the hunte hadde at him envye

Thus he that stood / in every manys grace
And in the kynges / hih benevolence
Was by envye / remeued / from his place
Lentyere in court / to haue noon assistence
So serpentyn was the violence
Which of this bern / sette the herte afire
Of fals malys / moor ire to conspire

Cause was ther noon / sauf that Lothbrok
Was more curyous / and gracious onto fame
Than was this hunte / and mo beestis took
In such practik / hadde a gretter name
Wherof this bern / laughte a maner shame
Gan compasse / of hatful cruelte
Whan he sauh tyme / avengid forto be

Upon a day / to hedir out thei wente
Unto a wode / sum game / forto fynde
And whil lothbrocus / no maner malis mente
This false bern / fil on hym behynde
And cowardly / the story makith mynde
Slouh hym right ther / in his furious teene
And aftir hid hym / among the busshes greene

The moordre accomplisshid / been tourned hoom ageyn
As he no thyng knowen hadde of the caas
And a day aftir / whan lothbrok was nat seyn
The kyng enquered / ech man where he was
And in this while / rennyng a gret paas
In kam his grehound / and fallne gan the kyng
ffil doun toforn hym / ful pitously whynyng

And whan the kyng hadde youe the grehound bred
Out of the paleis / a gret paas he ran
Streiht to his maister / where as he lay ded
And in this tyme / the kyng merueile began
And enquered / of many dyuers man
So longe absent / where lothbrok shulde be
Almost thre daies / that no man koude hym se

Wherof the kyng / fil in suspecion
Gan ymagyne / that it was not a riht
ffful diligently / made inquisition
Yif any man hadde had / of hym a siht
But on the molde aftur the thridde nyht
Onys ageyn / the grehound / dide appere
ffawnyng the kyng / with a ful pitous cheere

Wherupon / the kyng gan caste anoon
He wolde the maner fynde out and espie
Vnto what place / the grehound wolde goon
Cerchid out by prudent policie
Assigned a knyht / to folwe to that partie
In sekre wise / to knowe what it mente
Why so ofte / the grehound kam and wente

Afftir the grehound the knyht gan folwe a paas
Most secrely and maad therof no tale
By whom he kam there as Lothbrocus was
His vnder leues in a couert vale
His wounde bloody his face ded and pale
His eyen gastlelyh reuersid bothe tweyne
His hound a side which dide his deth compleyne

Moordre wil out thouh it a bide a while
Tyl his decert he must receyue his meede
ffor of this treson and fals compassid gile
The venymous roote began first of hatreede
ffor it was founde that Bern hath doon this deede
By certeyn sygnes and forto make a preeff
To knowe the trouthe the grehound was most cheff

Johan kynyt

When kyng Edmond hath fully apparceyued
ffro poynt to poynt / the mater how it stood
How this moedre / by Bern was first conceyued
Of fals envye / which maade his herte wood
And how to god / the doth than crye of blood
To doon of riht vengeance as him oughte
Vpon the traitour / that this treson wroughte

The kyng of riht / was meued to do lawe
To punysshe this deede / hatful and horryble
Bern was arrestid / which myht him nat withdrawe
Aftir conuict / by toknes ful credible
Deemt and iuggid / that in al haste possible
ffor to be lad / onto the same stronde
Wher first the bargee of Lothbrok kam to londe

Into that vessel the story is weel knowe
Which nouther hadde oore seil nor mast
Ffolwyng the cours what coost the wynd list blowe
Thus said bern be Iuggement was cast
Tween wynd and wawe his bargie almost brast
Ffordryue by rokkis and many hidous roche
Til toward denmark his vessel gan approche

And so befil of sodeyn auenture
As hap and fortune list for him purchace
With gret myschef the lond he gan recure
And was up dreuen in the same place
Wher lothbrocus was wont for his solace
To goon on haukyng whil he was alyue
Wher bern the hunte of fortune dide aryue

The bargie of lothbrok in denmark was weel knowe
But of his deth they knew no maner thyng
Nor to what coost the wyndes hadde him blowe
Nor what was falle of him that was here kyng
But fals bern at his up komyng
Was take anoon and lad forth by the hond
Toforn too prynces which gouerned al that lond

Hese prynces tweyne, sonys to lothbrok
Hynguar and Hbba callid in tho daies
In ful streiht wise the said bern they took
Of hym tenquere they made no delaies
Constreynyng hym bi rigerous assaies
To discure a mong his peynes alle
Of ther fadir what that was befalle

This cursid bern envyous and riht fals
And of complexion verray Saturnyne
Worthi to been enhaungid bi the hals
Or to be rakkid with a broke chyne
With face pale and tonge serpentyne
Reportid hath in his malencolie
How kyng Edmund slouh lothbrok of envye

And how this slauhtre was doon in despit
Of ther lyne, and of ther roial blood
That thei of haste, withoute more despit
Knowyng the deth of Lothbrok how it stood
To yeve ffaf credence, which that maad hem wood
Of herray rancour, and furyous cruelte
Caste on kyng Edmund, avengid forto be

Thus bi assent, these cruel prynces tweyne
Hyngwar and Ubba, of hatreed and envye
Thorugh al Denmark, proudly than ordeyne
To gadre in haste, al the chevalrye
Maad assemble, a passyng gret navye
Twenti thousend, of fyhtyng men thei hadde
Which bi the se, to ynglandward thei ladde

And bern the hunte / as ye shal vndurstonde
Vndertook the shyppis forto leede
Toward the costis of Estynttlonde
But eolus contrary was in deede
Which drof ther vessell to Berwyk upon tweede
At which port the story doth descryue
How that they weren compellid for taryne

Aftir this londyng / abrood they gan hem drawe
Thorugh al the North heldyng ther passage
And al the peeple that heeld of cristis lawe
They slowh hem up bothe old and yong of age
Cherches Abbeys they spoilid in her rage
ffully purposyng as the story seith
To slen alle tho that heeld of cristis feith

These woode prynces / these tyrantis most cruel
To god contrarie / and to lawe of nature
Be tytle of wil / as any tigres fel
To moedre and robbe / spared no creature
Certeyn yeres / there thei dede endure
Void of al mercy / and good conscience
No right pretendyng / sauf wil and violence

After tyme / of certeyn yeres space
Euer enduryng / in ther fals crueltie
Hyngwar purposid / forto chaunge his place
left vbba stille / in the north contre
And took with him / a passyng gret meyne
Toward estyngland / yf it wolde auaile
Of fals presumpcion kyng Edmund for tassaile

And with his meyne / ther he his tentis pikt
In sondry placis / where he dide hostele
The peeple oppressid / Durst nat with him fikt
Nor in no wise / his biddyng disobeie
Thus by force / this tirant gan werreie
The innocent peeple / by strengthe & myhti hond
Thoruh every contre of Estyngelond

This was the maner / of him and his men
Of every age / to slen alle tho he mette
Nother spared childre / nor women
Pite nor praier myhte nat his swerd lette
Thus procedyng / it happed that he sette
His pavelions / upon a pleyn contre
Which stood nat ferr fro Thetforde the cite

And as I fynde he entryng in that toun
Of his komyng / the cyteseynes unpourveied
Sleyng the peeple / as he wente up and doun
ffor lik as sheep they stood alone unpurveied
Without an hed / dispers and eek deneyed
And as beestis / with swerd of venjaunce
Thei were oppressid / and koude no cheuysance

Thus first the tyrant in his malis shewde
By cruel venjance the cite despoilyng
He spared no sect/sauf he kepte a fewe
Of folkes olde/vnweeldy and haltyng
Vpon ther feth/for febilnesse lanchyssyng
Such as he dempte/platly forto seye
That were not worthy/on his swerd to deye

This tirant Hyngwar by feer gan them compelle
Voidyng delaies forto teche hem where
Or in what castel kyng Edmund dide duelle
And of his puissance thei gan also enquere
And that thei shulde conueie him and lere
Toward the place or feten him a tuyde
Where his houshold/that tyme did a bide

ffor verray dreed/these folkes feeble and olde
Of ther lyues/stondyng in Iupartye
Vnto Hyngwar the place anoon thei tolde
And with his host/thei lad him that partye
Wher as kyng Edmund with his cheualrye
Withynne castle/a place delectable
His houshold heeld/ful roial and notable

But whan kyng Edmond knew of his comyng
And of the paynymes the maner herde seyn
Manfful lik a knyht he made no taryeng
But with his power stuffly weel beseyn
Beside Thetforde he mette him on a pleyn
Ther wardis set and shettrons in bataile
Euerich than other ful mortaly assaile

From the morwe that the larke songh
Whan in thorient phebus shoon ful bryht
Thei first assemblid on outher party stongh
And so contynued in ther mortal fyht
The slaustre last til it drouh to nyht
For with his knyhtis that kyng Edmond ladde
Of paynym blood ful gret plente he shadde

Edmond that day was cristes champion
Peuynyth him silf a ful manly knyght
Among sarseynes he pleied the lion
ffor they lik sheep fledde out of his syht
Mauhtre the danys he put hyng war to flyht
ffor wher his swerd that day dide tspede
Ther was no paynym asseen him durste a byde

The soil of slauhtre steynyd was with blood
The sharp swerd of Edmond turnyd red
ffor ther was noon that his strook withstood
Nor durste a bide asseen him for his hed
And many a paynym in the feeld lay ded
And many cristene in that mortal strif
Our feith defendyng that day loste his liff

Out of the feeld hyng war is a goon
With his meyne whan it drouh to nyht
Ded in that bataile abood ful manyoon
And blessid Edmond as cristes owne knyght
Gan to considere in his owyn siht
And streyhtly peysen this holy kyng most good
What perile folowth to shede so moche blood

Withynne him sylff he dempte of equite
Of paynym blood the gret effusion
Caused in soth thorugh ther iniquite
Perpetuelly ther dampnacion
And how in helle was no redempcion
And of cristene thoughte of verray trouthe
To seen such slaughtre it was to gret a routhe

Though he was bothe manly and vertuous
And a good knyght his story thus deuyseth
Yit of prudence this kyng victorious
In his memorie narwely aduertisith
How good conscience ageyn slaughtre aryseth
Wherfore of purpos avow he made in deede
Neuer his lyff no blood to sheede

He hadde a routhe that goddis creature
Which rassemblid his liknesse and ymage
Sholde in helle eternal peyne endure
Thorugh mysbeleue for paynymsyne rage
Considered also it was to gret damage
Wheen too peeples to seen such mortal stryues
Soules to ieuparte and losse eek of ther lyues

Ofte in his mynde and his remembraunce
This pitous mater was tournyd up so doun
Sempte onto thos it was ther displesaunce
To seen of blood so ther effusion
Makyng an heste of hool affeccion
Duryng his lif as hym thoughte it deu
ffor cristis sake shedyng of blood tescheu

Remembryng also hou cryst upon a cros
Lyst shede his blood our ransou for taquite
And of his power the thridde day aros
By mercy only with pes men to respite
ffor euer in pes he doth hym most delite
ffor which kyng Edmond his corage hath applied
To leue the werre and be with pes allied

ffolwyng the traces of our lord Jhu
Which loued ay pes and list no man wereie
Dexauple of whom with pes took his issu
Withynne his herte to close hym vndir keie
Which forto keepe he redy was to deie
And whil the kyng in pes thus doth soiourne
To speke of Hyngwar my stile I wil retourne

This chaptre declarith the title
of the martirdam of Edmond
the kyng of Estynglans

Whan cruel kyng War mayntre al his myght
Constreyned was the feeld to forsake
And with his meyne was I put to flyght
A dedly hatreed than in his herte awake
Hym to purveie a vengeance forto take
And heerupon a Werm most serpentyne
Of fals envye than in his herte myne

His folk disparpled, he than ffadere a theyn
To make hym strong, dide his diligence
Eek of his myscheff, Whan Olba herde seyn
Worth ten thousend, kam to his presence
Cruel of herte, bothe of oon sentence
Conspired in haste, of frowbard cursidnesse
By way of vengance, kyng Edmond to oppresse

Tofore therfore, bothe of oon assent
Of marcial pride, and pompous fel outrage
Thei heeld a coursel, and therupon han sent
Unto kyng Edmond, a surquedous message
By them devysid, contrary of langwage
Theron concludyng, a sentence ful perverse
Undir these woordis which I shal reherse

First in al haste foorth goth the massager
Sent by Hyrugwar, a ful froward knyht
Malencolius of face, look and cheer
Of port despitous, and coleryk of syht
Doyng no reuerence to maner wiht
Sauf to the kyng, knelyng he gan abrayde
In fel language, and thus to him he sayde

The myhti prynce, most victorious
On lond and se, of power inuyncible
Most to be drad, most marcial most famous
Notable in conquest, more than it is credible
Whom to descryue, it is an impossible
My lord Hyrugwar, as thou shalt vndirstonde
By me, of trust sent to the this sonde

He chargith the, and yeueth the counsail
Tobeie his preceptis, and therupon tabide
And the comandith to thi grret auail
Ffor thi sauacion, asseen to prouyde
Al thyng contrary, forto sette a side
That shulde rebelle ageyn his hih puissance
And the submytte, vnto his ordynance

This eek his wil/ that thow nat maligne
To disobeie his lustis/ in no thyng
Into his hand/ thy kyngdam to resigne
To paie a tribut/ and vnder him be kyng
And eek thow mustest/ accomplisshe his coynyng
Thy roial tresours/ and thy richesses olde
With him to parte/ of ryght as thou art holde

Ouer al thyng/ this charge on the he leith
And the comandith/ shortly in sentence
ffirst to forsake/ of Cristen dam the feith
And to his goddis/ that thow do reuerence
To offre onto them/ with franc and with encence
Be weel auysed/ thow make no delay
Al this taccomplisshe/ and sey nat onys nay

And he ageynward/ of his magnyficence
Shal to the ffrante/ a statly fayr guerdon
Assygne tresour/ onto thy dispence
And vnder him/ regne in this regioun
To these requestis/ make no rebellioun
ffor yif thou do/ thou shalt lese in this stryff
Thy kyngdam first/ thy tresour and thy lyff

Loo heer

Loo heer theffect of myn Ambassiat
to the I haue nomore in charge to seyn
Thy conseil tak of folk of hih estat
Shortly concludynge and lese no tyme in veyn
What to my lord I shal reporte ageyn
mak no delaies of that we han in hande
Rehersse in substance wherto he shal stande

The kyng nat rakel but of hih prudence
As he that was discret manly and wys
lyst for noon haste lese his pacience
Though he this mater sette at litil pris
Yit he purposed to heere and se thauys
Of a bisshop which that stood beside
By his conseil an answere to prouyde

The bysshop stton dynth in a perplexitte
At such a strett/ what was forto seyne
ffor of discrecion he pleynly did se
lyk as thenbassiat dide his witt constreyne
How this matier requered oon of tweyne
Outher tendure for short conclusion
void of al respitt/ Deth or subieccion

Toward the kyng/ with a ful pitous cheer
The said bysshop gan to tourne his face
Which for astonyd of this sodeyn matteer
koude yeue no couseill in so short a space
Such mortal dreed gan al his look dyfface
That he vnnethe had no word to speke
Til atte laste/ thus he gan out breke

To holde a feeld/ ye stonden Inpurueied
Heer atte hand/ your enmy is bataillid
Yif his requestis of you be disobeied
Your castel heer is lyk to been assailid
Of men natt stuffid nouther weel vitaillid
And of too harmys/ at so streiht a prykke
It were wisdam/ to chese the lasse wykke

ffro cristis feith / so that ye not flitte
Hool in your herte / that it be conserued
By dissymlyng / ye may your self submytte
Sithe the kyngdam shal to you be reserued
And that your lif / may be fro deth conserued
Your silff submyttyng / ye may dissymyle and feyne
ffor a tyme / til god list set or deyne

This bisshop hadde / a ferful tendirnesse
A Jelous dreed / in his ymagynatiff
Seyng the matter / stonde in such streihtnesse
As inpartie / of the kynges liff
Knewh no diffence / nor preseruatiff
As for the tyme / in his opynyou
Nor noon auoidance / sauf symulacioū

Bitt blissed Edmond / was not born to feyne
Yt longyd not / onto his roial blood
His herte eueron / departed not on tweyne
Hatis too heedis / closid in oon hood
So stable and hool / withynne his soule he stood
By manly force / of o face and of o cheer
Caste otherwise / to gouerne this mateer

He was endewed with alle the giftes seuene
Of tholigost this cristes champion
Of hooly feruence cast up his look to heuene
And inly syhhed of hih deuocion
Void of al feynyng and symylacion
Lyk goddis knyht manly dide abraide
Unto the bisshop euene thus he saide

Sere bisshop sholde I me now withdrawe
Shewe by dissymylyng a maner variance
fforce to put of with force is good lawe
But this mater requereth in substance
To be peysed more iustly in ballance
What sholde profite to my concyence
Wynne al this world and to god doon offence

Ther is in soth a nothir cheuysaunce
Heer in this world for thynges temporal
And a nother ghostly purueiaunce
Touchyng the thynges that been celestial
ffor werdly men iuparte lif and al
Slen ther neyhbours only to gete good
But god is lawe forbit sheedyng of blood

This proude legat of this tirant seith
And first purposith in his lettarie
That I sholde forsake cristes feith
And falle falsly in tapostasie
Submytte my crowne and my regalie
Aftir these thynges were fro me withdrawe
To cerymonyes of paganysmes lawe

But ther anoieth noon aduersite
Where dampnacion hath noon interesse
Of frowhards malys nor of Iniquite
ffor alwey trouthe al falshedes shal oppresse
Tirantis may reyne and floure in ther richesse
As for a while floreshyng in ther seson
Til thei vnwarly go to dampnacion

And for my part, al lordshepe set a side
To cristes feith, to which I haue me take
ffor lyf or deth, theron I shal a bide
Vnto my laste, and neuer my lord forsake
Which on a cros, deied for my sake
So for his loue and feith, to hidre in deede
I wil weel suffre my blood for him to sheede

And heerupon, this kyng most ful of grace
Most pacient, and most benigne of cheer
hys thoddis knyht gan to tourne his face
Sitget auys, towards the massager
That kam from kyngisbar, and bad him neyhen neer
Ley to ere, to herkne in pleyn langage
A ful answere touchyng his massage

Go to thi lord in al haste possible
To him reporte pleynly as I see
As for answere stable and most credible
Hold cristes feith I neuer shal dysobeie
But for his sauve spende my blood and dere
Syk my beheste Whan I Sathan forsook
And of his feith the stole and rynge I took

Thi lord beheseeth thre thynges onto me
This kyngdam Which that I do possede
And of his tresour he grauntith me plente
But of his richesse god wot I haue no neede
And of my lif I haue no maner drede
Sauf I wolde for my most hertis ese
Rathere lese al than onys god displese

And out of subieccion With al extort seruyte
In cristes feith I stonde at liberte
Mauhne thi lord and al thi proud sanguyte
Shedyng of blood and al mortalite
Causid of werre shal be left of me
And cristes lawe to meynteyne and diffende
With humble suffrance my lif I wil dispende

This proude knyht aforn from kynngesbar sent
Ys tournyd ageyn of inclynacion
And hath reported the kynges hool entent
How he wil neuer thorugh no collusion
fforsake his feith by no condicion
But rathere to been forto seie in wordes fewe
With sharpe swerdis on smale pecis hewe

The paynym sect he hath in hih despit
To submytte hym he demeth it were outrage
Blood forto sheede he hath noon appetit
And to been armyd he hath left his corage
Affermeth platly and seith in pleyn langage
He moost desireth a boue al wordly good
ffor cristis feith to dele and spende his blood

And to ffranchise his kyngdam and contre
He hath a corage that he hym self a lone
So his peeple myht stonde at liberte
To suffre deth meekly in his persone
More with the world he wil nat haue to doone
His manly knyhtis his soudiours nyh and ferre
Pes to cherisshe he hath yeue up the werre

Han that kynyng war this answere vnderstood
With men of armys passyng a gret route
He doid descendith as any tygre wood
And hath the castell beseged al aboute
Of whom kyng Edmond stood no thyng in doute
ffor cristis loue list no diffence make
But of hool herte to deie for his sake

He list nat suffre that no man sholde lette
The seid tirant nor make no diffence
Nor that no wiht the yatis sholde shette
ffor which in haste bi sturdy violence
Blyssid Edmond was brouht to presence
Affor the tirant sittyng in his estat
Lyk as was cryst whilom tofor pilatt

This kyng war first / with furious contynance
His couert malis / began thus to vnclose
Of cristis feith / with every circustance
Most cruelly / he than hym to oppose
Hym comaundyng / withoutyn any glose
fforto declare / and nat a poynt withdrawe
Yif his profession / were maad onto that lawe

Certes quod Edmond / I wol weel that thou knowe
To crist al hool / with body and herte
I am professid / what wynd that euer blowe
That fro his feith / I shal neuer dyuerte
ffor lyf nor deth / for ioie / nor for smerte
But so contynue / in every auenture
Withoute chaung / whil that my lif may dure

ffor ther is nouther tresor nor richesse
Regne of erthe al the pocessious
Power of prynces and ther pompous noblesse
With al the manacis of tirauntis and felouns
Thy furious thretis thyn adulacious
With al thy puissance shal me nat remeue
ffro cristis lawe nor fro his iust beleue

Thow maist thi swerd whette sharp and keene
And me dismembre ioynt fro ioynt assonder
lyk a tirant in thi contagious teene
me disseuere pecemeel heer and yonder
But triste weel and haue heerof no wonder
It passith thy myht and pompous violence
In cristes feith to arte my conscience

And o woord first as I the tolde
As I be than so I wil perseuere
my feith my baptem iustly I wil holde
Vnto my laste and so enduren euere
ffro my profession I wil departe neuere
Thow maist manace and slen my body heer
my soule franchised fer from thy power

Do thi beste thi rychesses I despise
Thow shalt of me han no subieccioñ
Nor fro my lawe restreyne me in no wise
To make me halte in my profession
And herkne a woord in short conclusion
Of my body though thow haue victorye
my soule shal lyue and regne with crist in glorye

In my Diffence I haue set a strong feeld
Vpon a grond of longe perseuerance
Of cristes ferth Deuysed a myhti sheeld
Ghostly swerd whettid with constance
And a clos brest of hope in my creance
Of loue and Dreed my body for tassure
Hool vndepartid shal be my coteaermure

A spere of trust vpward erect to heuene
Squared the hed fferth hope and charite
Which shal reche aboue the sterrys seuene
To he that lord bothe on too and thre
Vnto whos grace I submytte me
And for his sake as I oughte of ryht
Redy to deie as his owyn knyht

And for his loue / to suffre passion
I am maad strong / with herte / wil and cheer
The paleme of victory / as goddis champion
It to conquere / whil that I am heer
Of cristis cros I sette up my baneer
Sewauple of martirs / which with ther blody hertis
Gat heuenly tryumphes / al clad in purpil shertis

Thus I desire for to been arrayed
As a meek seruant / to seë my lord tapere
ffor hym to suffre I am nat dismaied
Thy god / my makere / my saueour most entere
Which with his blood / bouȝt me so dere
And sithe for me he suffred so gret peyne
To deie for hym / allas why sholde I feyne

Wherfore Hymyȝbar / make heerof no dellaies
ffro cristes feith I neuer shal declyne
Thy thret / thy manaces / nor al thin hard assaies
Shal for no dreed / withynne myn herte myne
And myn entent / at o word to termyne
As cristis knyȝt / of hool herte I defie
Alle fals goddis / and al ydolatrie

Off this langage kyngthar wex nyh wood
Made the kyng stronghly to be bounde
And comandid assern hym as he stood
ffirst to be bete with shorte battis rounde
His body brosid with many mortal wounde
And euer the martir a mong his peynes alle
Meekly to Ihu for helpe he than to calle

The cheeff refuge and supportacion
In his suffrance was humble pacience
Loue to his herte / gaff consolacion
With gostly feer / quekid the feruence
ffor charite / feelith no violence
ffor wher charite / afforceth a grette
There is of peyne / founde non outrage

The cursid tyraunts of newe cruelte
This martyr took most gracious and benigne
Of hasty rancour bounde hym to a tre
As for ther marke to sheete at and ther signe
And in this wise ageyn hym thei maligne
Made hym with arwis of ther malis most wikke
Resemble an yrchon fulfillid with spyrys thikke

He was the martyr seynt Sebastyan
Bothe in our feith lyk of condicions
Red by his sides the vital blood doun ran
And euer to Jhū he maade his orisons
Thus with the tryumphes of ther passions
Blissid martres with crownes laureat
Cleyme sith in heuene to regne in ther estat

Saÿntys/with arwes hookyd sharp and trowde
Spenten ther shot/ferser than lions
most mortally/as wounde/ay upon wounde
Renewid ageyn/the deepe impressions
What shal I write/of cristis champions
Which whilom thou3te/it dide her herte good
To wasshe ther stolys/in the lambis blood

In heuene bi trace/they cleyme to haue an hoom
ffolwyng the traces of crist that is ther hed
Which lik a geant/descendid from Edom
And hadde in Bosra/his clothis died red
Which feedith his knytes/with satryd wyn and bred
Set at his table/in the heuenly mansion
That drank the chalis/sheer of his passion

And among martirs/pleynly to termyne
With his harnement/died red as blood
Edmund was pressid/with strepis in the vyne
Vnto a tre bounde/whan he stood
To torn and rent/with withes that were wood
And thorwh perssid/euery nerff and veyne
Thynkynge for crist/to suffre/was no peyne

This mene

This mene while whan kyng war did him se
And sauh his body stekyng al in red
He maade his knyhtis rende hym fro the tre
And comanded to smyten of his hed
But the holy martir of oo thyng took first heed
Requered a space to maken his prayer
And most devoutly saide, as ye shal heer

Lord god which of beneuolence
Thy blissid sone sentist to erthe don
To been incarnatt for our gret offence
And of our trespas to make redempcion
Upon a cros suffrede passion
Natt of our merit but of thyn high pitee
ffro Sathanys power to make us to go fre

Now graunte me lord of thy magnyficence
Of thyn high mercy and benyngnyte
In my dyeyng to haue meek pacience
And in my passion forto graunte me
By meek exaumple to folwe the charite
Which thow haddist hangyng on the roode
Whan thow list deie for our alder goode

Now in myn eende graunte me ful constance
That I may deyen as thy trewe knyht
And with the palme of hool perseuerance
Parfourme my conquest only for thy riht
That cruel hyuy war which stant in thy siht
May neuer reioise nor putte in memorye
Of my soule that he hatt victorye

Vnto tyrantis ys nott victoryous
Thouh they thy servantis slen off fals hatrede
ffor thylke conquest is more glorious
Wher that the soule hath of deth no dreede
Now blyssid ihu for myn eternal meede
Only of mercy medlyd with thy ryght
Receyue the speryt of me that am thy knyht

And with that woord he gan his nekke enclyne
His hed smyt off the soule to heuene wente
And thus he dyed kyng martyr and virgyne
In gostly feruence so hoote his herte brente
His liff his blood for crystys sake he spente
Such heuenly grace god list vnto hym sende
With grace he gan with grace he made an ende

Anys of despit the body ther forsook
A glorybus tresour of gret worthynesse
But of the martyr the holy hed they took
And bar it forth of froward cursidnesse
In tacouert shrowded with thyknesse
Of thornys sharpe the story makith mynde
And ther they hid it that no man shulde it fynde

But blissed Jhū which every thyng may se
His holy martir listnott so forsake
But of his grace and merciful pite
Knowyng that he deied for his sake
Suffred a wolf his holy hed to take
And to conserue it ageyn assautis alle
That foul nor beeste sholde vpon it falle

An vnkouth thyng and straunge ageyn nature
That a beeste furyous of felnesse
Which of custum doth ay his bestial cure
With mannys flessh to staunche his gredynesse
But now he hath forgoten his woodnesse
And meekly lith awaytyng nyght and day
Vpon the hed as for a synfuler pray

Thus kan the lord his martyrs magnefie
Of his goodnesse with many fair myracle
The rage of beestis appese and modefie
Ageyn whos myht may been noon obstacle
Which hath heer shewid a wonderful spectacle
That a fers wolff bamaner obseruance
To serue the martyr list doon his attendance

But to his myht no thyng is inpossible
Danyel was sauff among the fers lyoun
Seyn John baptist recorded on the bible
Lyued in desert mong serpentis and dragouns
And among crystis myhty champiouns
Kyng Edmond hadde his story seith the same
A wolff to keepe hym ther was no lamb more tame

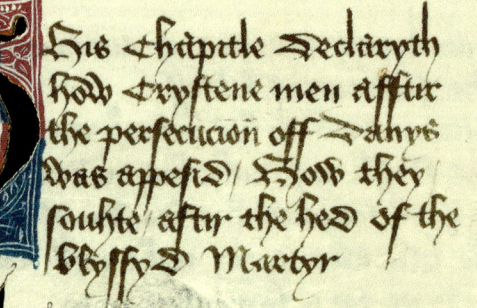

This chapitle declaryth
how crystene men afftir
the persecucion off danys
was apesid / How they
souhte aftyr the hed of the
blessyd Martyr

Han slayn was the dreedful tyrannye
Of cruel hynguar in this regiou[n]
That he and Obba with al ther chevalrye
With drough in party ther persecucio[n]
The crystene peeple of hih devocion
Assemblyd wern fully purposyng
To seeke the body of ther holy kyng

And compleyned / atwwen hope and dred
Whan they hadde / his blyssid body foude
That they wanted / and failed of the hed
ffor which they wepte / with syhhes ful profoude
Sekyng the forest / and the valys roude
With blast of hornys / with rachesse & with howdys
Thorugh Heylesdone / serchyng al the woddys

And by a maner replicacioñ
Ech onto other / gan crye in ther walkyng
Wher is our confort / our consolacioñ
Wher is allas / the hed now of our kyng
This was ther noise / with sobbyng and wepyng
Allas, allas / that we be thus destitut
Of our cheeff ioie / our blisse and our refut

Suffre us onys / beholde thy blyssid face
And seen at leiser / thyn Auncelyk visage
Bowe thyn eeris / to our compleynt be trace
fforto relese / our constreynt / and our rage
Allas Edmond / appese now our damage
And to our compleynt / of mercy condescende
ffor noon but thow / our myscheuys may amende

The lord of lordys celestial and eterne
Of his peeple hauyng compassion
Which of his mercy ther clamours kan conceerne
Relesse ther langour and lamentacioun
Herde of his goodnesse ther inuocacioun
And gaff hem comfort of that they stood in dreed
Only by grace to fynde ther kynges hed

With wepyng terys, with vois most lamentable
So as they souhte walkyng her and ther
Where artow lord, our kyng most agreable
Wher artow Edmond, shew vs thyn heuenly cher
The hed answerde thryes, her, her, her
And neuer cesid, of al that longe day
So for to crye, tyl they kam where he lay

This heuenly noise, gan ther hertis lyhte
And them releue of al ther heuynesse
Namly whan they hadde, of the hed a syhte
Kept by a wolff, foryetyng his woodnesse
Al this considered, they mekly gan hem dresse
To thanke our lord, knelyng on the pleyn
ffor the gret myracle which that they haue seyn

They thouhte it was a meruele ful vnkouth
To heere this langage of a dedly hed
But he that gaff into the assis mouth
Whych speech of old, rebukyng in his dreed
Balaam the prophete, for his vntoodlyheed
The same lord, list of his grete myght
Shewen this myracle at reuence of his knyht

Men han eek rad / how in semblable cas
In bokes olde / make mencyoū
How that an hert spak to seynt Eustas
Which was first cause of his conuersioū
ffor god hath power and iurysdiccioū
make routhis speke of bodies that be ded
Record I take of kyng Edmondis hed

Off this myracle that god lyst to hem shewe
Some wepte for ioie / the story berth witnesse
Vp on ther cheekys / terys nat affewe
Distillid a dow of ynward kyndnesse
They hadde no power ther sobbyngis to represse
When ioie and sorwe / by sitnes out shewyng
How greet entiernesse / they hadde vnto ther kyng

Thus was ther wepyng / medlyd with gladnesse
And ther was gladnesse medlyd with wepyng
And herthly sobbyng / meynt with ther swetnesse
And soote compleyntes / medlyd with sobbyng
Accord discordyng / and discord accordyng
ffor for his deth / though they felte smerte
This sodeyn myracle reioisid ageyn ther herte

The folkys dide ther bysy dilligence
His holy tresour, this relik souereyne
To take it up with dew reuerence
And bar it forth til they dide atteyne
Unto the body, and of thylke tweyne
To gydre set, god by myracle anoon
Enioyned hem that they were mad bothe oon

Off ther departyng/ ther was no thyng seene
Atwen the body/ and this blissid hed
ffor they togidre/ fastnyd were so cleene
Except only/ Who sotylly took heed
A space apperid/ breede of a purpil threed
Which god list shewe/ tokne of his suffrance
To putte his passion/ more in remembrance

The said Wolff/ in maner gan compleyne
That he so hih a tresor/ hath forgo
To saue the martir/ dide his besy peyne
Wolde in no wise/ departe the body fro
Of bestial loue/ felte a maner woo
fforto disseuere/ thouhte a gret penance
ffro thylke thyng/ Where stood al his plesance

It is no meruelle/ the beeste was not to blame
Though he were wo/ to parte fro his richesse
Which ageyn nature/ maad him to be tame
That to no man/ he shewed no fersnesse
Tyme of theueguyes/ compleynyng his distresse
And meekly aftir/ to Woode wente ageyn
Most doolfully/ and was neuer aftir seyn

Unto the body of this gloryous kyng
Beside the place where he dide endure
Anoon at Oone a place of smal beldyng
They ful deuoutly maade a sepulture
Whos martirdam by rewrd of scripture
Was tyme of yeer as I can remembre
Upon a monday the moneth of Decembre

In which day the moone was of age
Too and twenty by computacion
Indiccion tweyne reknyd in our langguage
Eyhte hundrid yeer fro the incarnacion
And seuenty ouer, as maad is mencion
Whan the holy martir was by a contis cleer
Day of his passion of age thretty yeer

On which day his legende maketh memorye
He suffred deth and cruell passion
And with a palme celestiall of victorye
Be grace is entrid the heuenly mansion
Hymuyth a tryumphe most souereyn of renon
As kyng and martir wher he may not mysse
Eternally for to regne in blysse

Goth glorious martir which of gret meeknesse
ffor crystes feith suffredist passion
Abyde my penne enlumyne my rudnesse
To my dulnesse make a direccion
That I may vndir thy supportacion
Compile the story hangyng on this matere
Off seyn ffremond thyn owyn cosyn dere

Thoruh thy fauour I cast me for tassaye
To declare of humble affeccion
How seyn ffremond be myracle dide outraye
Hynguar and Hubba thoruh his hih renoun
And them venquysshid in this region
ffirst write his liff and thereupon procede
As god and grace list my penne leede

Folwen myn Auctour that wrot his liff toforn
In frensh and latyn of gret auctorite
Off the twurthe gadren out the corn
And voide the chaff of prolixite
Reherse the merueiles of his natyuyte
Aftir to forward how he dide him quyte
A litil prologue afforn I wil endite

Incipit vita sancti ffremundi Regis et martiris Edmundi carissimi consanguinei qui eiusdem martiris interfectores vnd inuitante prostrauit graciose vna cum miraculis Edmundi inde martiris aliterdicti prout in post sequentibus clarius elucescit.

Ho kan remembre the myracles meruellous
Wich crist Ihu list for his seyntes shewe
Or who kan write the tryumphes glorious
Of his martirs in nombre nat a fewe
And I am ferful aboue myn hed to hewe
Lyst frowhard chippis of presumpcion
Sholde blynde myn eyen in ther fallyng doun

Yt is nat holsom to looke ageyn the sonne
For dirked eyen dulled of ther syht
Men symply lettryd that but litil konne
Sholde feerful been in herte of verray ryht
To entermete of thilke eternal lyht
Which bryhtest phebus in ordre sette hym selue
Myd his crowne of the heuenly stones twelue

The charboncle of his nature red
And cerawnius lyk the fyry leuene
Wolde oppresse and dirke a dullyd hed
fforto beholde ther bemys sent from heuene
The cours celestiall of the sterrys seuene
To comprehende ther dyurnal meuyng
To bareyn wittis is a ful strange thyng

And yiff the cleernesse of the heuenly sterrys
So fer transcende the liht of this parties
Thempire abouen that from vs so ferr ys
Wher the nyne ordres in ther thre Jerarchies
Preisen the lord with ther soote Armonyes
What mortal man the liht may ther discerne
But grace be guyde to leede him and gouerne

God hym silff in thilke emperial se
Ys souereyn sonne that paleys tenlumyne
Lampe lanterne and liht of that cite
Wher non eclips may lette his bemys shyne
To for whos face and throne that is deuyne
Heuenly spirrtis in his laude and preisyng
Neuer cesse Osanna for to syng

Ther the felashepe of heuenly citeseyns
Queer of prophetis and patryarkes olde
Twelue Apostlis as Juges souereyns
Which cristis lawe in erthe tauhte and tolde
And ther also men may seen and beholde
Gret multitude of martrs clad in red
Steyned in cosra to dere they hadde no dreed

The prothomartir seyn Steuene with his stonys
The fyry gredile ther shewid of Laurence
And holy Vyncent his flessh brent to the bonys
On colis rede by extort violence
Denys of Grece thoruth meek pacience
At mountmartir slayn in his constance
Sent by seyn Clement to conuerte ffrance

George Cristofre myhty champiouns
Off crist Jhū suffred for our feith
Ignatius that tamed the lioun
In his passion as the story seith
Blyssid Elsaȝ his hed to wedde he leith
Was natt ferfull to chaunge this present liff
With crist in heuene to be contemplatiff

The holy man ycallid seynt Albon
prothomartyr off this region
Suffred deth sythen ful yore agon
ffor crystes sake and bitter passion
Sitt now to mynde cometh the champion
Off Estynglond born of the Saxon lyne
Callid seynt Edmund kyng martir and virgyne

The holy kyng / of his liff most cleene
This cristis knyht / hardy as lyon
Was for our feith / shet with arwes keene
As I toforn / haue maad mencion
Now purposyng with supportacion
Of al the martirs aforen rehersid heer
Induce a story / longyng to this mateer

How that a cosyn / of this hooly kyng
Callid Fremundus was manly and notable
Ful merueilously / by grace of martyryng
Ordeyned was / this story is no fable
Vpon Hynguar / for to be venjable
And afteryn Obba / which in ther cruel rage
Hadde slayn his vncle tho thretty yeer of age

In this mateer toforn as I you tolde
Because it is / onkouth and wonderfull
My spirrtis feeble / and feynt with yeeris olde
And my corage appallid / and maad dull
Myn eyen derkid / and with the mystes full
This to seyne / the myst of onkonnyng
Troubleth my wit / to writhte so hih a thyng

I resemble vnto Polypheme
That hadde oon eye set in his forhed
Nat lik Argus of siht I kan not deeme
Which causith me allas whan I take heed
That hand and penne quake for verray dreed
Of which paklsy but grace be my leche
Me to directe I not who shal me teche

Who shal speke or telle the grete myht
Of our lord god or shewe his gret power
Al his preisynges reherse as it is ryht
Or synge his laudes with nootis fressh and cleer
Most merueillous and vnkouth fer and neer
Shewde in his seyntes as auctours alle accorde
Ffrom our stoty the trouthe kan recorde

Ful wonderful was his concepcion
Shewed by myracle and tokyns manyfold
For atteyn kynde as maad is mencion
A child that was but of thre daies old
Thorugh goddis myght hath of his berthe told
And ouermore myn autour seith the same
Prophesied what sholde be his name

The child baptised anoon was affter led
Callid hym ffremund by his mouth toforn
And anoon affter by myracle who take heed
That no signe befiled were nor lorn
Vpon that nyht when ffremund was born
Saies myne the story doth us lere
Ouer the paleis a reynbowe dide appere

Whos thre colours yiff men list to knowe
Gaff first a tokne and bar greet witnesse
The wattry greene shewed in the reynbowe
Off chastite disclosed his clennesse
The saphir blewh his heuenly stabilnesse
The hardy red apperyng in the skye
His marterdam dide signefie

Ioyned by this bowe quatreble of colour
Thus ouerspred be many fer contre
That he was born to been a gouernour
Worth sceptre and swerd by roial dignyte
Weryng a crowne ordeyned for to be
Seyn miscreautis to his encres of glorye
Lyk a conquerour to haue of them victorye

And as myn auctour, doth also for him seyte
He hadde in thre, a prerogatyff
ffirst of the heuene, a treble preuylegye
Don to be made, duryng al his lyff
ffoulde of his doctryne most contemplatyff
To teche his sogettis, dide upon him take
And affter martyred he was for cristes sake

His ffader, his mooder, lik as the story seth
By myracle he maad hem be baptised
And by his techyng, he turned hem to our feith
And affter that, so as it is deuysed
fforsok his kyngdom, and affter hath praktysed
With ffrut and rootis of verray parfitnesse
Space of seuene yeer, to lyue in Wildirnesse

And al this tyme his clothis wer nat old
With other tilleyne leued as an hermyte
And by his Wacchyngis, and fastyng manyfold
Be side a Welle lay lik an Anachorite
Whos berthe and lyff, fayn I wolde endite
Compendiously, and writen the substance
But a ffals serpent callyd Ignorance

Troubleth my penne I may not foorth proceede
But grace shal helpe the wedir forto cleere
And these too knyhtes do favour in this neede
ffirst blyssid Edmund and his cosyn deere
Callid ffremundus to conveie this mateere
And undir support of these seyntes tweyne
To write this story I shall do my peyne

God by ther praier shal be my supportour
Help me forward yif it be his wille
By influence of his mygty socour
Into my penne sum licour to distille
Licour of grace my purpos to fulfille
Under whos mercy and helpe that he shal sende
Off this story to maken a good eende

Off Burchardus folwe I shall the style
That of seyn ffremund whilom was secretarye
Which of entent dide his liff compile
Was his registrer and also his notarye
And in desert was with him solitarye
With him ay present remembryng every thyng
Wrot liff and myracles of this holy kyng

To kyng Offa ffremund was sone and hayr
Reynyng in mershlond the story berth witnesse
His moodir Botild riht goodly and riht fayr
And a woman of met parfitnesse
Longe bareyn the story doth expresse
And she was suster and lik in many a thyng
Unto seyn Edmund the holy glorious kyng

The kyng the queen wer ferr rone in age
And al this while Botild was bareyn
Tryst and hevy lest ther heritage
Wer translatid to som hayr foreyn
ffor lak of yssu but god be grace hath seyn
To ther requestis the maner and the guyse
Ceriously the story shal devyse

IN that provynce / withynne a smal village
Ther dwelled a man / which callid was Aldave
Which with his wyff / in a smal cotage
Ther houshold keeld / whos bylode was but bare
And as the story / in ordre shall declare
She hath conceyued / myn auctour writ the same
Born a sone / and Thobie was his name

The thridde day / of his natyuyte
Ageyn nature / the story listnat lye
Be myracle / ffamous in that contre
The said child / gan speke and loude crye
And be amaner / vnkouth prophecye
How kyng Offa / as the child hem tolde
Sholde haue a sone / in his daies olde

And ouermor / in pleyn language he seith
Whan he wer born / how he sholde also
ffader and mooder / conuerte vnto our feith
By goddis myght / and many a meruelle do
And sike folkys / shall lowly come hym to
To fynde socour / of euery maladye
And he be grace / shal soon hem remedye

Cure leprys / and folkys that be blynde
With newe liht / he shall hem enlumyne
To furious men / he shall yiue wit and mynde
And sturdy hertis / to grace he shal enclyne
Tourne mescreantis / by his prudent doctryne
To crystes lawe / and make creplis goon
Delyuere his kyngdhm / from al ther mortal foon

And he shal be kyng/ martyr and virgyne
And in tokne/ that al this thyng is trewe
A reynbowe/ shal shewe daies nyne
Vpon his paleis/ with fressh beemys newe
And euer a lyche of colour/ and of hewe
And contynue in oon/ his glad lyht
Whan he is born/ and dyrynge the same nyht

Holde openly a mong the folkes alle
ffor a signe/ to putte al in certeyn
How al the peeple/ ffremund sholde hym calle
That no tokne/ shewid were in veyn
And how his mooder/ that was afforn bareyn
Sholde ber a child/ be grace of god sent dun
Which sholde enlumyne al this region

And whan the child/ hadde alle these thynges told
Beyng of age/ but only daies thre
He gan requere/ with cryeng manyfold
As alle folkes myhte heere and se
In the name off the Trenyte
Be baptised/ in presence off echon
Affter his baptym/ gaff up the speryt anoon

The tyme approched/ and faste upon hath hied
The Qweeen conceyued/ be grace of Goddis myht
Lyk as the child/ toforn hath prophesied
The reynbowe affter/ appered anoon ryht
And Daies nyne/ shewed a brood his liht
To sygnefie/ a sonne was sent don
That sholde enlumyne/ al this regyoun

As newe greyn/ out off feeldis olde
And leues greene/ growe out off trees gray
And as the bawme which in wyntres colde
Seepe in the groud/ which in the roote lay
Upward ascendeth/ in Apreylle and in may
So semblably/ from Offa and Botyld
Be grace off God/ conceyued was this chyld

When Jhu was born, old was Elysabeth
And old also was hooly Zacharye
The blissid tyme, to mete in Nazareth
Whan in the mountayn, she mette with marie
And thus by grace, and sperit of prophecie
Whan kyng Offa, and Botyld, were bothe old
Off ffremundis burthe, toffern a child hath told

Affter whos berthe, for short conclusion
As myn auttour, in ordre hath deuysed
Whan he to yeeris kam of discrecion
Off bisshopp Oswy ffremund was baptised
And in monyth crystene the feste solempnysed
Ech man for Ioie, syngynth in his desire
Laude and preisyng, be to the trenyte

To teche the peeple, ffremund, dide excelle
And them conuerted, from ydolatrye
Off cristis baptem, fulled hem in the welle
The feith off Ihu, temsance and maynesie
And his soietis deuoutly, gan hem hye
Gret multitude, alle off oon assent
Off hooly baptem, to take the sacrament

The kyng the Queen, in ther daies olde
Be hooly ffremundis, informacion
Lyk as the child, be prophecye tolde
Hou by ther sonys, predicacion
Off feithful herte, and humble affeccion
They shulde receyue, in ther Rial estat
Baptein be ffremund, and be regenerat

thus

Thus be the grace off our lord Jhu
ffro day to day the trouthe was weel seene
ffremund encresshed fro vertu to vertu
As any sonne his fame shon so sheene
Wrouhte myracles made leprys cleene
The grace off god dide hym so magnefie
That he cured euery malladie

His fadir offa feeble wex for age
And blissid botald his moodir most benyngne
As they that gan approchen to the stage
Off decrepitus expert be many a sygne
By prudent counsail cast hem to resygne
Sceptre and crowne with al the reyalte
To yonge ffremund the kyng Osm forto guye

The herte off ffremund to god so strong was knet
In cryst Jhu stablisshed his plesance
To serue the lord he thouhte it was weel bet
In parfitnesse be long contynuance
Than haue in erthe royal gouernance
On the peeple heer in this present lyff
Sithe he hym caste to be contemplatyff

But ther ageyns/ ther was so gret instance
That yonge ffremund/ sholde be crownyd kyng
As trewe enheritour/ by goddis ordynaunce
Sonde fro the stok/ off kynges descendyng
The ye de gre/ by lyneal conueyyng
He next in ordre/ cronycles who list rede
Affter his ffader/ ordyned to succede

Off his persone and off his stature
Was noon so likly/ that tyme doutles
ffirst considered/ his Royal engendure
His hooly liff/ his vertuous encres
Cheryssher off concord/ louere off trouthe and pes
All thes thynges/ peised in his persone
Dempte hym most worthy/ for to regne allone

Vois off ryche and vois off the poraylle
And hool the noise/ gostly and temporall
Was noon so hable/ to haue gouernaylle
As was ffremundus/ born off the stok royall
And thus the clamour/ bothe off oon and all
By many reson/ alle off oon entent
To regne as kyng/ made ffremund to assent

The feeste yholde, and the solempnyte
Off his notable coronacion
Nat withstandyng his Roial Dignyte
He aduertised, off prudence and reson
How that al worldly dominacion
Hath in erthe, but a short abydyng
Nouther off Pope, Emperour nor kyng

On hooly bookys/ his lust was forto reede
Redressed all wrongys/ sustened rihtwisnesse
His hand mynystre/ to almesse deede
Cheryshynyt presthod/ for ther holynesse
Off maidnes widwes/ supportyng the clennesse
Hauyng compassion/ on euery poore wiht
Ay moore enclynyd/ to mercy than to riht

And whan he hadde reyned but a yeer
By goddis grace/ feruently enspyred
Saith hool ther was/ no trust in this liff heer
Off gostly loue/ his herte was thoruh fyred
Toward desert/ so soore he hath desyred
fforsook the world/ and al his reyioun
And took his weye/ toward carlion

Thoughte hool it was to his goostly auail
ffader and mooder off purpos he forsook
With other tweyne that were off his counsail
On the se syde a litil barge he took
And as it is remembred in the book
Withoute vitaile or worthy purueance
Commyttith his passage to goddis ordynance

Vtreth the se, parteth fro the stronde
With wynd ydryue, fyue dayes to and fro
Withouten oore or wyndyr kam to londe
Off auenture, that tyme it happid so
Vp an yle, frowardr to kome to
To wikked spiritis, a place conenable
Lyk a desert, off ffolk inhabitable

Yet in that yle, ther were ful fayre mounteynis
Rennyng reueres, and wellis crystallyne
Large meedwis, and lusty greene pleyns
Trees ylade, with holsom frutys fyne
And I suppose, by grace which is dyuyne
By god ordeyned, for ffremund in to dwelle
With his too feerys, beside a plesant welle

And Ilsefaye, men that yle calle
Off old tyme, desolat and sauage
More agreable, than was his royall stalle
To hooly ffremund, though he were yong off age
And ther he bilte, a litel hermytage
Be side a ryuer, with al his besy peyne
He and his fellawis, that were in noubre tweyne

A lytil chapel he dide ther edefie
Day be day to make in his praiere
In the reuerence only off marie
And in the worsheype off hir sone deere
And the space fully off seuene yeere
Hooly ffremund, lik as it is founde
Leued be frut and rootis off the grounde

Off frutis wilde, his story doth us telle
Was his repast, penance for tendure
To stanche his thrust, drank watir off the welle
And eet Acornys, to sustene his nature
kernellis off notis, whan he myhte hem recure
To god alway, doyntih reuerence
What euer he sente, took it in pacience

The olde serpent hadde at hym enuye
By many frowarD fals suggestion
Brouht onto mynde, his stat, his reialye
Off tyme passid, his dominacion
And gaff to hym, ful many occasion
For tattruchichid, but he off hool entent
Gaff thank to god, off al that euer he sent

Fer hungyr, thrust, excesse off hoot or cold
Nor for no constreynt, off aduersite
Nor for assaut, off temptacion manyfold
In hym was founde, no mutabilite
Stable as a wal, he stood in his desyre
Al worDly thyngis, bothe in herte and thouht
ffor cristes sake, ffremmys sette at nouht

To cristes plouh/he hadde set to hond
Off hih perfeccion/and list nat looke ageyn
He was nat wery/to tourne amyd the lond
His gostly trauaile/for to spille in veyn
Gruchchyng/nor feyntise/was neuer in ffremud seyn
But lyk a champion/in erthe sent from heuene
That slouh the serpent/with his hedis seuene

His cloth hool/conserued by myracle
Duryng seuene yeer/fressh as the firste day
What god wil saue/ther may be non obstacle
Nor geyn his wil/ther may no man sey nay
Thus hooly ffremund/parfit at al assay
ffor in desert/lyk cristes olden knyht
Ay off oon corage/perseuereth day and nyht

And whil that he/doth in desert soiourne
In abstynence/and contemplacion
To kyng Offa/my style I wil retourne
And of purpos/make a digression
ffor in that tyme/the book makith mencion
Ynggwar and Hbba/with danys aryuyng
Slouh seynt Edmund/martir maide and kyng

fforn rehersid / his lyff his passion
ffor Cristes feith / how he shadde his blood
By meek suffrance / and humble affeccion
Bounde to a tre / meekly whan he stood
Shet with arwis / off tirantis fell and wood
With many a wounde / hedid and dismembryd
As in this book / is heer toforn remembryd

Hys brother in lawe, for verray impotence
Off crokid age, sorwful in his entent
That he was feble to make resistence
Whos lusty yeeris were wastid and y spent
His counsail took, his massageris hath sent
To seeke ffrenduns, bothe nyh and ferre
Ageyn the Danys, to make a mortall werre

Too and tweinty massageris notable
Off preuyd men, men off discrecioun
Which as kyng Offa knew weel that were able
To seke and serche thoruth al this regioun
And alle straunge yles abouten envyroun
And smale prouynces enclosed with the se
To fynde a place wher ffremund sholde be

But at the laste, only by goddis grace
And off his merciful dyuyne prouydence
They were conueied, and brouht vnto the place
Where as they fond, off ffremund the presence
In lowly wise, dyde hym reuerence
Vnknowe to hym, but in ful pleyn langwage
They mekly tolde, theffect off ther message

And benyngnely, ther massage to aduertise
Afforn declaryd, his ffadrys benyson
And affter that, they than in ordre allegge
The rewmys myscheff, the desolacion
Off paynymes, the thrux oppression
Crystene lawe, lowhe put vndir foote
ffremund requeryuth, to socoure and do boote

With wepyng eyen, also they hym tolde
Off cristis lawe, fynal destruccion
Maidnes rauesshid, men slayn that were olde
Cherchis robbid, dispoiled and bordun
Menstris desolat, reuersid up so doun
Al religion, and clerkly disciplyne
With furye off danys, brouht vnto ruyne

Crystene feith, brouht to destruccion
The seuene sacrementis, hangyng in Iupartye
Ryht was Iuste, powder extorsion
And fforce allas, tornyd to robberye
ffully concludyng, ther was no remedye
In al thys myscheff, to saue this wofful lond
But grace off god and ffremund ley to hond

In this mater, meruellious to here
Seynt ffremund, stood in a perplexite
Gan to chaunge face, look and chere
Caste in his herte and peised thynges thre
His ffadres meschef, the danys crueltee
And cheff off alle, he dradde for his partye
Lyft newe intrusion, brouhte in ydolatrie

Considered also, in what plight that he stood
In his profession, for to lyue solitarye
Teschewe werre and shedyng eek off blood
ffro which entent, he cast him not to varye
And to been armyd, he thouhte that it was contrarye
ffor an hermyte, that hath the world forsake
Deedis off armys for to vndyrtake

Thus al been theyne hangyth in ballance
Most specially o thyng he ran to dreede
The furious Ire the vnmercifull ventance
Off paynymes swerd cristene blood to sheede
But in this cas for his eternal meede
He was ay redy off hool affeccion
ffor Cristes feith to haue suffred passion

And forto sette alle thynge in seurte
Off conscience the wyndes forto cleere
And cloudy mystes off ambiguyte
Hooly ffremund took hym to praiere
Besouhte the lord off hool herte and enteere
That off his power most mercyfull and benyngne
What he shall do to shewen hym som signe

The nexte nyht, an Angell dyde appere
Whyl he slepte, and by avysion
Sad that he sholde been off riht good chere
And haste hym hom in to his regyon
Be strong in speryt lik crystes champion
The creauntis off Denmark for to werreye
And cryst Jhu shal for the feeld purveye

With two and twenty, from his fader sent
Off chose persones, in this Ambassiat
Noubred tho tweyne, with ffremund ay present
Made foure and twenty, notable off estat
And hoo be grace, made hem fortunat
And ech of them, thorugh goddis grete myht
Sempte a thousand, in ther enemyes syht

Amevyd be grace, maad in vertu strong
Wher god helpith, ther doth no force faile
Gan haste hem forth, ther passage was nat long
Took a smal shyp, hadde redy arryuaile
Gan haste hem forth, toward ther bataile
Ffond his fader, wepyng whan he beheeld
With cristene peeple, oppressid in the feeld

Sitt whan

But whan Iustyner, herde off ther komyng
To hooly ffremund, an heralde sente down
Grantyng hym, withoute more taryyng
In pes and quyete, to haue pocession
Under his lordshepe, off al that region
So he wolde crystes feyth forsake
And so tabyde, and to ther lawe hym take

O ff whiche sonde ffremund hath despit
Not for the kyng whiii to which he hadde ryht
But for our feith withoute more respit
He seide he wolde aquyte him lik a knyht
And in the name off hym that hath most myht
Crist Jhu approche he than towarD
The paynym party displaies his standard

Forn alle other fyrst ffremund dide assaile
He proude Danys crist Jhu was his guyde
Hew assonder fersly plate and mayle
His manly knyhtis ay fyhtyng be his syde
Afforn ther face no paynym myhte a byde
And foure and twenty that day withoute obstacle
Slouh fourty thowsand only be myracle

To cristis power no thyng is impossible
So as him lyst he may the feeld ordeyne
As moyses remembryth in the bible
Levitici affermyng in certeyne
How that an hundryd to speke in wordes pleyne
Sholde off ten thowsand as put is in memorye
Be goddis grace haue the victorye

For he allone may his conquest shewe
Wher as hym lyst off his magnyfycence
With gret nowmbre or ryht with a fewe
Al oon to hym ther is no difference
And to conclude breffly in sentence
Nat fro the erthe by mene off spere or sheeld
But he be grace yeueth conquest in the feeld

Thus this champioun this knyht most vertuous
Hooly ffremund dide the feeld recure
At day on Danys he was victoryous
And afftir that he dide off his armure
Kneled douñ and dide his besy cure
Thanked God by ffull grett avys
And off his conquest to hym he gaff the prys

Duryng this werre ther was oon Duc Osby
With kyng Offa a prynce off thet estat
A dyssymyler which ful traytoursly
ffro Crystes feith was a fals renegat
Afforn with Inguar sworn and confederat
By vndirmynyng this was his menyng
Afftir ffremund he to be crownyd kyng

Compassyng þat hooly man shal deye
And be mordrid by som fals tresoun
And therupon to fynde a redy weye
His labour was by som occasioun
And as seyn ffremund kneliþ lowhly doun
Thankyng the lord for his gracyous speed
Affter his victory Oswy smet off his hed

And sodenly his hooly chast blood
Ran lyne ryht in to the visage
Off this tretour as he be syde stood
Brent hym so sore þat he fyl in rage
To heer the guerdoun off his mortal outrage
Lo how þat god off ryhtful Iuggement
Kan punysshe the mordre off folkis Innocent

He furye off Osbẏ was so importable
At saue the deth, he sawh no remedye
But off this morder, be cause he was coupable
Vnto seyn ffremund, fill lowde he gan to crye
Mercy O martir, haue mercy or I dye
With wepyng teerys, and with a sobby sown
Off me most wrecchid haue compassiown

My grete offence to the I am a knowe
My sclandrous gilt, my trespace most horryble
Which haue deserued, to brenne in helle lowe
My transgressioun, allas is so terryble
But ageyn mercy, no thyng is Impossible
O blessyd martyr, rewe on my trespace
That kan no refut, but fle to the for grace

Ther fil anoon, a wonderful myracle
By mercy shewyd vnto this woful wiht
At whos request, ther was no long obstacle
But that his praier was herd anoon riht
The hed off ffremund, by grace off Goddis myht
Wher as it lay, dide sodenly abrayde
And vnto Oswy euene thus it sayde

Cristis Apostel/Which hath off crist power
And grace to graunte/thy lows peticion
He graunte to the off hool herte and enter
Off alle thy synnes/an absolucion
And me receyue/in his confession
To liff euerlastyng/so that my meek suffrance
Accepted be/to his deuyn plesance

And as it is remembryd/in historye
And regystred/be old antiquyte
Beside Radforde/he hadde this victorye
On them off Denmark/lord blyssid moot he be
Which off his merciful/dyuyn mageste
Made foure and twenty/but a fewe in noubre
ffourty thowsand/Danys/to encoubre

Off this myracle the fame ran ful wyde
The triumphe rad/with lettres aureat
The palme up born/long ordeyned/for tabyde
Theternal chaplet/off branches laureat
Crownyd for ther meryt/with capital purpurat
Ordeyned for martirs/with many a riche ston
And a mong alle ffremund was set for on

His blyssid martir, by myracle up aroos
Afforn predestynatt to liff that is eterne
Took up his hed with his tweyne handis cloos
Whos hooly steppis to sueye and to gouerne
As folkis present myhtte weel discerne
By supposaile he woynnt forth so ryht
He was conueied be trace off Angellys myht

Aben Whytone and Harborough he aboos
And ther I fynde, a while he dide dwelle
Took his swerd, and evene ther he stoos
Toucheth the groud, and ther sprong up a welle
With crystal watrys, the strenys ran up welle
And wessh a way the blood that was so red
Which dow distyllyd from his hooly hed

Took off the watir, ffolk sawh that were present
And whan he hadde wasshe cleene his woundis
Tournyng his face toward the Orient
Beside the welle, where yit the groud is
And passed natt, the sylue same boundis
Hasff up the host, he knelyng in that place
Toward the hevene, with cheer erect and face

Aby with othre rehersid heer beforn
Took up the body and the holy hed
And to Offcherche ffremund they haue born
With his sherte closyd strewte in led
And with deuocion dilligence and dred
Withynne an arche a twyxe two pillerys
They mured him up wher he lay many yerys

Wrouhte myracles and many sondry sithes
His fame spred in many fer contres
And in this lond ther were thre virtynes
Which that hadde dyuers Infirmytes
Oon was podagre in handis leggis knees
A nother inwet the thryde who lyst lere
What euer was sed she myhte no thyng heere

Off these virgynes, the story doth us teche
The firste Elfleda, namyd off these thre
Which hadde lost the office off hur speche
Thous the seconde, hadde this infirmyte
Off hand and foot, she fayled liberte
This to seyne, the cely poore wyht
Potayre was, myhte not stonde up ryht

The thyrdde mayde and the laste off alle
The cronycle recordith in substance
men in that tyme cryhteda dyde hir calle
And lak off heryng was al hir penance
But for to fynde relees off ther grevance
Though alle these thre were severyd fer assonder
Ther dreem was oon and that was a gret wonder

They hadde in charge by revelacion
These thre in noubre hou they sholde hem dresse
Toward Offcherche which is a kouth tou
In Warbyk shire the story beryth witnesse
Ther to fynde relees off ther syknesse
A specyal sygne yove to hem by grace
Wherby they sholde approche vnto the place

To the sepulchre off ffremund wene vpryht
As the aungele by myracle dyde hem leve
Ther sholde a skye as any sonne bryht
Dresse up his bemys to the sterrys cleere
Lyk Phebus tressyd in his mydday speere
Neuer dyrken nor noon eclypsynge haue
Tyl on to tyme they kam vnto his graue

Thus conueyed be bryhtnesse off the skye
Off cherche as maad is mencion
Wher off ther syknesse they fond furst remedye
And affter that by reuelacion
Off the Angel they hadde instruccion
To take the body and the hooly hed
And karye it with hem out off the cas off led

And as the story doth in ordre telle
These thre virgynes retourned been ageyn
Sam to a ryuer that namyd was Charubelle
And faste by they fond a ful fayr pleyn
And sye they wolde no thyng were in veyn
ffor the hooly martir off alabastre whit
They dyde ordeyne a toumbe off gret delit

Ther in was graue the Natyuyte
Off crist Jhu abouten enuyron
The riche presentis off the kynges thre
ffeste off candilmesse receyued be Symeon
His meek suffrance his Resurreccion
In which toumbe they haue fully purposid
That the body off ffremund shal be closid

AND on this pleyn passyng fair to seene
Beside this ryuer be cause it drouh to nyht
They took a yerde off sallow with leuys greene
Markyng the place and set it ther vpryht
And toward morwe whan the day was lyht
They kam ageyn anoon as they arose
To burye the body holdyng ther purpoos

Bllt they

But they fond / nouther the body nor the ston
Nor no tokne / ther off koude see
Saue the yerdes / left there whan they were gon
Was growe that nyght / in to a large tre
ffor which the maidnes / that were in noubre thre
Gan sore weepe / and compleyne / for distresse
ffor losse only / off ther worldly rychesse

God saw how sore the absence dide hem greue
Off hooly ffremund / in ther affeccion
He off his mercy / ther compleyntis to releue
Maad hem to knowe / by reuelacion
How by dyuyn disposicion
He / by myracle / and gracious auenture
Prouyded hath / for his sepulture

And ther affter they sholde no more enquere
But pacientlyh suffre ther penance
With glad herte and with ryht good cheere
meekly abyde goddis ordynance
ffor thorugh his myhty gracious purueyance
He shal ordeyne be mysteryes ful profounde
A tyme prouyded whan he shal be founde

But wher he lay the pleyn that was a lofte
Was plenteuous off floures and pasture
The gras the herbys holsom smothe and soffte
And vertu hadde nat only be nature
But be myracle syk beestis to recure
ffed with the hay or gras in his grennesse
They were maad hool off newe or old syknesse

The place was had in gret reuerence
Off alle folkis that dwellyd faste by
Worshepyd it with al ther dilygence
ffor myracles that fille sodenly
And to declare the grouud and cause why
I doute not al was doon be grace
Off hym that rested in that hooly place

Than fil it so, a pilgrym off this Reelm
Callid Edelbertus, the story tellith heere
Beyng present at Iherusalem
So as he lay, with hool herte and entere
At the Sepulchre knelyng in his prayere
Upon a nyght hadde this avysion
To haste hym hoom toward his regyon

Callid by name, the cronycle maketh mynde
Thre sondry tymes, Wynne nyght be nyght
And he desired, alwey as I fynde
Beyng in doute, thoughte in his inward syght
What may this been, I conceyve nat a ryht
Prayyng god, devoutly ther knelyng
What was his will, to have ful knowlechyng

The thrydde tyme wher as this pilgrym lay
Hadde in precept / no lengere for to dwelle
By goddis cheef / but in al haste that he may
Haste hym homward / myn auctour doth thus telle
Toward the ryuer / that callid is charwelle
And on that pleyn / to forn as is maad mynde
He sholde off Salowh / a large tre ther fynde

Vnder which / the hooly seynt was graue
Blyssid ffremund / afforn heer put in mynde
Tolde hym toknes / which that he sholde haue
At his komyng / the place for to fynde
And oon ther was / which was nat lefft behynde
Which sholde be shewid / to hym the same day
Amyd the place wher as the martir lay

Thylk whyt Sowhe / cloos vnder the treene
Entre nor yssu / noon shewed on the pleyn
With younge pigges / in noubre ful thretteene
A ful gret pas / komyng hym a geyn
And for to putte al thyng in certeyn
Withynne a chapel / be side that soil ful blyue
He sholde fynde / notable preestis fyue

Alle these toknys rehersyd poynt be poynt
To Ethelbertus breffly in sentence
The Angel pullid his ryht arm out off Ioynt
Ffor crokid bakward for his diffidence
And manacid for his neclygence
Neuer to been hool til vpon the day
That he kam thedir wher seyn ffremund lay

Gretly affraied with his infirmyte
ffelte in his arm gret peyne and passion
Took streiht the weie to Rome the cite
To this entent for short conclusion
Ther to receyue ful absolucion
Be Cristus vyker what so euer falle
Off his offence and his synnes alle

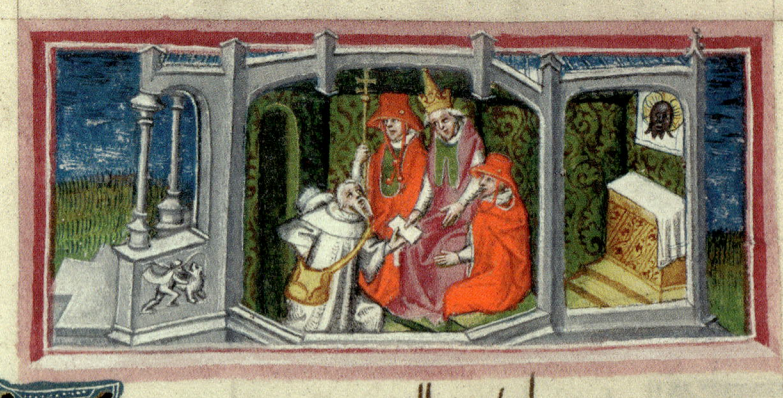

And to procede and telle forth the caas
ffor good expleit / touchyng his wurne
To the pope as his purpos was
He goth in hasste for mor auctorite
And with a spirit off humylite
Sette a side al long dilacion
Ech thyng commyttyng to his discrecion

Off these materes remembryd ceryously
Maad to the pope a declaracion
Touchyng these myracles in ordre by and by
Which thyng conceyued / off such discrecion
Bad hym resorte hoom to his regyon
Delyuered hym lettrys / notable and special
To speede his purpos testymonyal

Han he kam hoom With sullis auctoryses
He dilligently made Inqursicion
Ffond alle the tookyns trewe affter dewysed
Aboute the place off his Inuencion
Helthe off his arm and restitucion
The sowthe the puttis god lyst so prouyde
And preestis fyue dwellyng ther be syde

So the Bysshop off the diocyse
Made off his bullis presentacion
Callyd Gyrynus / which in goodly wyse
Assentyd is to his translacion
Took certeyn prelatis off relygion
And by the Popis ful auctoryte
Translatyd hym to Dunstaple ye may se

To which place the body whan they brouht
Be goddis grace, and his grete myht
Sondry myracles, the hooly martir wrouht
made folkis lame for to goon vpryht
Cured leepres, to blynde men gaff syht
And remedye, to syke folkys alle
That for socour, vnto his grace calle

Holy ffremund, martir mayde and kyng
On to seynt Edmund, cosyn most entere
Which wrouhtest myracles, heer in thy leuyng
With crist now regnyng, a boue the sterris clere
Socoure thy seruantis, by mene off thy preiere
And ouer them hold thy gracious hond
And saue forth e Walk his peple, and al this lond

Whilom off Danys thow haddest the victorye
By myracle, as maad is mencion
Now crownyd martir, in the heuenly consistorye
Geyn gostly ennmyes, be our proteccion
Prey specyally, for al this region
ffor to preserue, fro damagis this contre
Our feithful trust is in thyn vncle, and the

For semblably as thow kyng ffremund
Hengwysshe deft Danys at Ratforde on the pleyn
Riht so thyn vncle the hooly kyng Edmund
To saue this lond fro trybute in certeyn
At Geynesborugh by myracle slowh kyng Sweyn
The which story accomplysshed of old date
I am purposid in ynglissh to translate

Thowsand yeer vii hundred and thretten
Folwyng crystes Incarnacion
Mortal constreynt an importable teene
Troubled al the lond off brutus Albion
Beyng that tyme kyng off that region
Etheldredus which by accountis cleer
Was off his kyngdhm the fourte and thretty yeer

This newe trouble than off stryves olde
By them off denmark which off antiquyte
Cast with this lond a werre forto holde
Off wilful malice and compassid crueltee
As in cronycles men may reede and se
Which to contynue with strengthe and myghty hond
Kyng Sweyn off newe is entred in this lond

Ydle was ther noon but wilful tyrannye
By a maner off newe Intrusion
Be Sweyn conspired cleymyng the regalye
Off danys ryht to haue pocession
He ffer to regne cleymyth by succession
Entryng this lond the story lyst seen
Be extort power gan to brenne and sleen

Spoiled menstres, and holy cherches brente
Robbed cites, and euery famous toun
And for a tribut, thorugh al the lond he sente
He list off pryde make noon excepcioun
His swerd off venytance whet be extorcioun
Off hatfull yre and off furyous rage
Spared noither old, nor youth off age

In Etheldredus ther was no resistence
fforce to withstonde his cruel tyrannye
Riht was oppressid, by mortal violence
The kyng for feer fled in to Normandie
Thus desolat, void off al chevalrye
Stood al the lond, which gaff gret hardynesse
To the tirant, the peeple for to oppresse

To hooly places was do no reuerence
Men slayn and moordred, by venytable cruelte
Wyues oppressid, by sclandrous violence
Widwes rauesshid, loste ther liberte
Maidnes diffouled, by force ageyn ryhte
Preesthod despised, religyous in disdeyn
Be cruel hatrede off this tirant Sweyn

Took up on hym, for to be callyd kyng
Presumptuously, off force ageyn al ryht
ffil was his thrydde collusion his werkyng
His lawes gouerned, be power and be myht
Off rihtwisnesse, eclipsid was the liht
Gaderyng off tresours, be gold, to haue auayl
ffraude and falsnesse, wer cheff off his counsail

Sette a trybut general, on the lond
With couetyse, he was so set affyre
So fer off rauyne, he strecchid out his hond
The mor he gadred, the mor he doth desire
Sent his collitours, into euery shire
Spared nouther pleynly to deuyse
Conseruies off Seyntes, ffredam nor ffranchise

Gadris in haste, this tribut and talliage
Be rauynours and robbours infernal
To hyndre the poeple, by extort pillage
Delay excludid, mercy was noon attal
And for this tribut, was so general
To Englond, strecchid this wrytyng
Wher seynt Edmund whilom was crownyd kyng

The peeple nat vsed to be tributarye
Cleymes franchise off Edmund ther patron
The raueynours aletttyng in contrarye
Were importune in ther exaccion
The peeple a theynward for ther proteccion
Knowyng no refut as in this mater
Sauff to the martir to make ther prayer

Thus ryche and poore / off al that regioun
Off oon affection / with herte wil and myht
With deuout prayer / for ther redempcioun
Kam on pilgrymage / with sondry tapris lyht
To the hooly corseynt / ther wacchynge day and nyht
Besechynge hym / his seruauntus to socoure
A-geyn the tiraunt / that wolde hem deuoure

Which pacyently / acountyd ful ten yeer
Jngland hath suffryd / this tribut ful terryble
ffonde fauour noon / Gross nor particuler
Constreynt off rygour / was to hem odible
That to contynue they dempte an ympossible
By pouert spoyled / which made hem sore smerte
Which as they thouhte / craysshed at here herte

They lay prostraat / knelyng a-boute his shryne
Women yo barfoot / pitously wepyng
With letanyes / preestis dede enclyne
By abstynence the peeple lowh fastyng
Men off religion / be prayer and wakyng
Besouhte the martir / ther fredam to renewe
And off his mercy / on ther wo to rewe

Ther requestis were natt maad in veyn
ffor he that was cheeff cubyculer
Aboute seynt Edmund / and his chauberleyn
Alle off assent / dyde ther deuer
To prae ther patron / to caste his eyen cleer
His heuenly eyen / ther trouble to termyne
With liht off confort / ther hertis tenlumyne

Fyrst Ayllewyn / that cely creature
Afforn his shryne vpon the pauement lay
In his preiere / deuoutly dyde endure
Seelde or neuer / parted en nyht nor day
ffer whan so euer / his liges felte affray
The peeple in hym / hadde so gret beleue
Thorwh his request / Edmund sholde hem releue

The perfeccion off Ayllewyn was so couth
So renomed / his conuersacion
That many a tyme / they spak to gidre mouth be mouth
Touchynge hyh thynges / off contemplacion
Expert ful offte / be reuelacion
Off heuenly thynges / to speke in woordes ferue
Be ghostly secretys which god lyst to hym sherwe

And as.

And as he lay slepyng on a nyht
Clad in a stole off Angelik cleernesse
Whittere than snow / cloth dryd with sterrys bryht
Off cheer celestiall / ful mortuyng off fayrnesse
His sterryssh eyen lik phebus off fresshnesse
With plesant langage the martir than abraide
And to his chapleyn euene thus he saide

Go forth in haste spille no tyme in veyn
And looke thow do trewly my massage
And in my name sey thus to kyng Edwyn
That off my peeple he axe no truage
Ther ffranchise is to stonde in auantage
ffrom al trybut and al exaccion
Vnder the wynges off my proteccion

To doo nat my peeple suffre hem lyue in pees
Trouble nat the kalm off ther tranquyllite
In thy requestis be nat to rekleeff
To axe hem trybut yt longith nat to the
Ther ffredam stablysshed off antiquyte
Se that therfore off malys nor off pryde
Be vsurpacion thow sette it nat a syde

Thy wilful errour in thus to comprehende
Ys for to trouble me and my franchise
To make hem wronfully ther goodis to dispende
Be war therfore and werke afftir the wise
Vpon enbassiat that thow nat despise
ffor yiff thow do pleynly to expresse
God and I ther damages shal redresse

Toward mercie whan Chyldebyn a book
He was somdel abasshed in his wratthe
O Ceynesborugh the ryht way he took
God was his guyde to forthren his viage
And for tacomplysshe fully his massage
Affter the fourme off his instruccion
He folwed theffect off his auysion

He dide his massage openly declare
To the presence whan he kam off Sweyn
ffro poynt to poynt / list natt oo woord to spare
Whom for to heere / the tirant hath dysdeyn
Bad hym devoyde no mor ther to be seyn
And departyng thouh that it was late
Toward nyht he wente out att the gate

Destitut he was off herbergage
Sauff ther beside a cherche yeerd he took
Mongh graue stones / thouh he was old off age
He leyde hym doun and nyh almyht he wook
And toward heuene ful ofte he caste his look
Prayeng the lord / to rewe on his symplesse
And toward morwe / be grace his iourne dresse

And for to putte this mater in memorye
Retournyng homward the story berth witnesse
At Lyncolne withynne the territorye
With slombre oppressyd / trauayle and heuynesse
ffor recreacion / his labour to redresse
Toward Auret the martir / mayde and kyng
To hym appered saide / as he lay slepyng

That newe trouble hath thy cheer disteynyd
With heuynesse consumed and apeyrid
Pluk up herte al that my peeple hath pleynyd
I shal redresse or thow be hoom repeyrid
Off my socour be nat dysespeyrid
Or ouht longe bet tydyng thow shal fynde
By whos support al I shal amende

Cellbynus resortyng hoom ageyn
At Gernesborugh the silue same nyht
In his castell to for the tirant Gweyn
Blissid Edmund armyd lik a knyht
Comeres by an Angel as Phebus cleer off lyht
Hes off Gweyn a sharp spere in his hond
Wiltow quod he haue tribut off my lond

Off heuenly colour was his cote armure
The sheeld azour off gold with crownys thre
In tokne he was by recurs off scripture
Kyng and martir his legende who list se
The thrydde crowne tokne off virgynyte
He with a spere sharp and keene thoruhe
Gaff the tirant his laste fatal wounde

Gweyn hadde his wil may be no respitt
Thus onto hym Edmund gan specifie
Haue thyn axyng haue heer thy tribut
Guerdon couenable Gweyn fals tyrannye
Gweyn afrraied loude gan to crye
Callys up his host I not what weye he took
But with the noyse al the castel shook

No man merueile off this onkouth myracle
That Sweyn was slayn in his chaubre a nyht
Geyn goddis power ther is noon obstacle
In heuene in erthe egal is his myht
As weel in derknesse as in the cleer lyht
His victorye with spere swerd or sheeld
In chaubre shewed as weel as in the feeld

To prudent peeple and folkis that be sad
Tween feeld and chaubre is no difference
Lytylwhat abedde his myht is to be drad
ffor cowardise hath noon experience
Wher he list use his myhty violence
In bed in chaubir in castel or in tour
The swerd al oon off his dredful rygour

Som ffolk nat wis to cowardise arette
That Sweyn was slayn in his bed a nyht
The castel cloos the stronk wal nat lette
But that his entre kam al off goddis myht
As thoruh a glas perce the bemys bryht
Whan phebus shyneth Sweyn in the same wise
Slayn be myracle and by no cowardise

And to procede as it komyth to mynde
This Egelwyn herde in his passage
A gret rumour off horsmen behynde
Which spak to hym in ful pleyn langage
Art thow nat he that brouhtest the massage
ffrom kyng Edmund thenbassiat not tretable
Dredful sodeyn hasty and vengable

As kyng Edmund saued fro tribut
This lond be myracle sette the Reuhm in pes
Ryht so the Danys off confort destitut
Durste affter neuer put them sylff in pres
To do no truage nor hold to ther encres
Wher God diffendeth lat us neuer drede
A theyn whos power no mahys shal procede

Off Sweynys deth thus writeth marian
Hou don Wolmarus born off gentil blood
Dowmb deff podagre and an Essex man
The same hour so with hym it stood
Lay a deuenth and his tyme abood
Which neuer spak erst sodenly abrayde
To his ffreendis euene thus he sayde

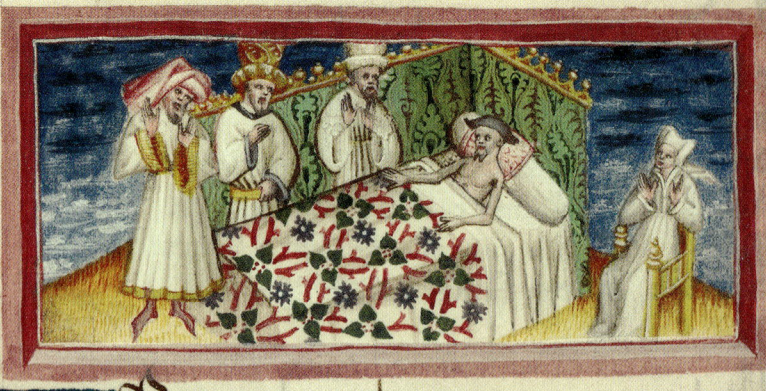

The sharp spere off kyng Edmund certeyn
Do sette this lond / fro tribut / in surnesse
Oppressid hath / the cruel herte off Sweyn
Wherby this lond / is brouht in gret gladnesse
These woordis says / the man in his siknesse
Yald up the gost / neuer afftir / nor afforn
And spak no moor / sithe tyme that he was born

Thus Egelwynus / be toknys ful certeyn
As he homward / than his Iourne holde
Hauyng relacion / off the deth off Sweyn
Withynne hym sylff / his herte than to bolde
And euery part / this myracle forth he tolde
Thanked god / off his gracious vesit
Which hath this lond / delyuered fro tribut

Fro the cronycle, yiff I shal natt varye
Kyng Sweyn was slayn, as maad is mencion
The day seconde, off frosty ffebruarye
A thousand yeer, fro the Incarnacion
ffourtene over, by computacion
The days affter saltyng his carevn
In to Denmark be sailed hoom ateyn

AND as myn Auctour in ordre doth deuyse
Neuer tiraunt durste putten assay
Off Seynt Edmund to breke the franchise
But he were punysshed withoute long delay
Hard is with seyntis for to make assay
Be example as I can weel preue
By Leoffstan which whan he was shyrreue

To seynt Edmund hadde no deuocion
To heere off hym frowhard by dysdeyn
Off his myracles ful smal affeccion
To heere hem rad the tyme spent in veyn
His libertes he was theragheyn
To sitte in Iugement he caste a certeyn day
Withynne the boundis wher the martir lay

A woman gilty fferful for hir trespace
ffor dreed off deth socour for to fynde
Off blyssed Edmund entred is the place
Lowhly besechynth he on hir wo taue mynde
Leoffstan dide hir arreste and bynde
By Cachepoll with force and violence
Un to the seynt doynth no reuerence

The clerkis present in devyn seruyse
Gan in maner to make resistence
Off hooly church, deffendyng the ffranchise
But al for nouht, ther was such assistence
By pres off baylyues, beyng in presence
With multitude, the clerkis to assaile
That to sey nay it wolde nat auayle

The offycerys rauynous lik houdnis
With leoffstan furious off chier
Off the cherche entred is the boudis
The clerkis prostrat lay in ther preier
The woman crieth that alle men myhten hier
Help blissid Edmund help and be my reed
ffor but thow helpe I shal in haste be ded

Keep and conserue thy Jurediccion
ffro this tirant or this day I shal deye
The clerkis knelyng in ther oryson
Keep thy ffredam, O martir, they gan preye
But leoffstan lyst nat for to obeye
Noth al his court is entred off entent
In the cherche to sitte in Jugement

No reuerence doon to the seyntuarye
The tirant was so vnmercyable
Be violence the woman forth they karye
A quest redy/ the Iurours Inportable
The woman crieth with voys ful lamentable
Help hooly martir/ shal I be this wise
Dempt in the boundis/ this day off thy franchise

The Iuge procedeth/ to execucion
Thouhte no ffredam a theyn hym sholde auayle
A ffeend a noon/ took pocession
Off this tirant/ sore dyde hym trauaile
In euery membre/ and in his entraile
Amyd his torment/ yald up his gost in hast
I dar nat deeme/ what way he is past

Thus kan the martir punysshe hem that been rebel
ffolk that truste hym conforte hem and releue
Socoure ther pleyntes supporte ther quarel
As this myracle openly doth preue
Who seketh his helpe shal natt mescheue
To his seruantis gracious and benygne
A tale for them a geyn hym that maligne

Knyhtes fyue off malice and rauyne
Ageyn the ffredam off Edmud ful coupable
Haberioyned and in platis fyne
Entred his court took hors out off his stable
With swerdis drawe to shewe hem sylff vengable
Yff any man wolde make resistence
Hadde forth the pray be extort violence

But sodenly thus with hem it stood
Or they passyd the boundis off the gate
Trauaylled with furye and echon wex wood
Repented affter offred up mayl and plate
Confessyd assoiled in cronycle set the date
Euer afftur off hool affeccion
Hadde to the martir gret Deuocion

Eek oon off fflaundres that was a fals brybour
Kam undyr colour off oblacion
Kyssed the shryne lyk a slyh pilour
And with his teth the book makith mencion
Rauhte off a nowche but in conclusion
His teth stak stylle and on the nowche abood
By myracle whler as the pylour stood

He koude natt remewe fro the place
But stylle aboode that alle men myhte se
The Couent kam prayyng the seynt off grace
Upon that wrechche for to haue pite
Loosnyd he was and wente at liberte
Thus kan the martir on rebellis be venytable
Whan they repente benygne and mercyable

Theuys eyhte tentre the cherche at nyht
Don broughte a laddere a nother broughte a barre
A nother besy with al his strengthe and myht
To vnpyke lokys a nother to vnbarre
Don with a leuour to leffte the doore on harre
Don with a pykoys a nother hadde a spade
Don clamb the wyndowe his fardell for to lade

Don at the thrownsel lowe than to myne
A nother besy to entre yiff he myhte
Compassed aforn tafe kome to the shryne
To bern a way the hold with stonys beyhte
But to ther malis the martir hadde a respite
So sore be vertu he dyde the theuys bynde
Tyl on the morwe the peeple dyde hem fynde

Stood stylle as ston sore in them sylff amasyd
Some with ther armys crompyd to the bak
With eye up tournyd a boute they haue gasyd
Don with his crampoxon a nother with his sak
Another stood and on the wal he brak
ffro ther werk myhte no remewe make
Tyl on morwe they were at myscheff take

                         Douze

Bounde and fetryd, and throwen in pryso͡wn
Tyl the Bysshop off the diocyse
Sat upon hem, dide execucio͡wn
By hasty vigour, procedyng to Justise
Hangyd they wern, shortly to devyse
Lo how the martir, the robbours dyde quyte
Off this mater, what sholde I more endite

The lawe he thoughte, yaff to hym licence
To execute, hasty Jugement
Be cause in cherche, was do the gret offence
Conspired be theuys alle eyhte off assent
Nat seyn afforn, this text baunsement
Cesse thow nat, thus thapostel bad
Them to delyuere, that to the deth be lad

Off whos deth, this bysshop Theodrede
Hadde al his lyff, herthy repentance
ffor this cruel, and this hasty deede
Made the peple faste and do penance
He sore contrit, tryst off contenance
Hadde euer ssyter, for that gret offence
Withynne hym sylff, remors off conscience

Han ffolk off pryde lyst haue no reward
To hooly seyntis, for to do reuerence
God punysscheth hem, recoord on seynt Edward
Whilom at Cesur, beyng in presence
Whan Osgothus off hatful neclygence
A lord off Denmark, lyk a wood man ferde
The myracles off Edmund whan he herde

Towarde the martyr he bar old hatrede
This Osgothus as it was affter founde
Despysed his myracles whan he herde hem rede
Yet he in ordre was callyd the seconde
Nexte to the kyng with gold and perlys rounde
Rychely beseyn and statly off array
Aboute the shryne walkynge al the day

Off coryouste and presumpcion
His look he caste towardes that hooly kyng
Off fals dysdeyn voyd off devocion
Depravede his vertues his passion his huyrnyng
And as he stood the martir thus skornynge
With a brood fawchon hangynge be his syde
Ffyl plat to grownde, mawgre at his pryde

God is nat plesed with such fals blasffeme
Doon to his seyntys off indignacion
Sauff to martirs which the lord to queme
Suffred for his sake deth and passion
To plexe with seyntys kometh off ambicion
Which god wil punysshe with vnhar venjance
Ffor which this story is put in remembrance

This lord off Denmark for al his gret bost
ffor al his tresour his gold and his perre
As a demonyak veryd with an host
fful ofte turmentyd in his infirmyte
The noise arose oon seith there lyth he
Tyl the rumour off cryyng heer and there
Kam be report to the knyhtes ere

Which thilke tyme in chapitle was present
Off his grace and Royall dignyte
With the Abbot and hool al the covent
Tencresse ther franchise and ther liberte
Off his benygne and mercyful bounte
Gaff hem the maner off mildenhale and the tou
With eihte hundredis in pocession

Al this tyme Osgothus lay dystreyned
In his furye walkyng up and don
Whan hooly Edward knew hou he was peyned
Off Royal mercy he hath compassyon
Heeryng the noyse and the horryble son
Dredful terryble off this wood man
Thus he seyde to Abbot Leofstan

Fader Abbot it longyeth to you off ryht
With hooly prayer and devout oryson
With al your covent to gon anoon ryht
To the holy martir in processyon
The letany song with devocion
Prayyng the seynt off his benygnyte
On thys Ostothius for to han pite

This myracle is the more auctoryssed
That seynt Edward was ther at present
Ouht off reson to be mor solempnysed
ffor the holy kyng was so dilygent
Off his trace to go with the covent
In procession ther knelyng on ther kne
To save Ostothius off his infirmyte

And by the counseyl off Wllyllabyn certeyn
To the fertre the syke man was led
And a gret space whan he hath ther leyn
Wher he afforn was furyous and mad
He than a slepe and to wede sad
Restoryd to helthe lowly down knelyng
Gaff thank to god and to the hooly kyng

Amende his maners he than eek blyue
Gette a syde his frowarde sturdynesse
To the martir durynge al his lyue
He was deuout / took to hym meeknesse
What vayleth pryde / what vayleth frowardnesse
Exemple heeroff ye may seen at the leest
Be vengeance take in Essex on the preest

Hych to the martir seyued herberygage
Lad by Alkelwyn to londene the cite
His place brent for his frowaro language
Penytance take men myhte the flawme se
But ther ageyn off grace and off pite
At Crepilgate entrynge that roial toù
Side many myracle the book maketh mencioù

Bosforn at Stratfforde callyd at the bowe
His litil carre whan it sholde passe
The breegge broke the deep strem vnknowe
Narwh was the plaunche ther was no weye but grace
Aboff the flood o litel wheel gan tpace
The tother wheel glad on the boord a lofte
And Alkelwyn wente afforn ful softe

He kam to londene toward eue late
At whos komyng blynde men kauhte sycht
And whan he was entred Crepylgate
They that were lame be grace they goon vpryht
Thouhtful peeple were maad glad and lyht
And ther a woman contract al hir lyue
Crryng for helpe was maad hool as blyue

Hire veer the martir heeld ther resydence
Tyl hyllysbyn be revelacion
Took off the bysshop vpon a day licence
To leede kyng Edmund ageyn to bury toū
But by a maner symulacioū
The bysshop graunteth and vnder that ȝan werche
Hym to translate in to Pollys cherche

Upon a day / took with hym clerkis thre
Entreth the cherche off seyn Gregory
In purpos fully / yff it wolde be
To karye the martir fro theuys peruysh
But whan the bysshop was therto most besy
With the body to poulle for to gon
It stood as fyx as a gret hill off ston

Multitude ther myhte noon auayle
Al be they dyde ther force and besy peyne
ffor but in ydel they spente ther trauayle
The peple lefte the bysshop than dysdeyne
Draught off corde nor off no myhty cheyne
Halp lyte or nought this myracle is no fable
ffor lik a mont it stood yliche stable

Wher upon the bysshop than meruaylle
ffully dysseraudyd off his entencion
And whan ther power and fforce gan to faylle
Wyllelbyn kam neer with humble affeccion
Mekkly knelyng sayde his orison
The kyng requeryng lowly for crystes sake
His owyn contre he sholde not forsake

With this preier Wullffryn aroos
Gan ley to hand, fond no resistence
Took the cheft wher the kyng lay cloos
Lefste hym up withoute violence
The bysshop thanne with dreed and reuerence
Conueyed hym forth with procession
Tyl he was passid the subarbis off the toun

Alle syke ffolk that for helpe souhte
To the martir lyggyng in maladye
Were maad hool, myracles euer he wrouhte
Who callid to hym ffond hasty remedye
Wher he passith, upon ech partye
Thorugh every toun and every smal village
The peeple kam to conueye his passage

Broke brenchis, they ttin a tteyn renedde
Strowed al the weies with floures fressh and grene
And with clothes off many dyuers helbe
They hengh ther wallis, maad the pament clene
That noon obstacle was in the weye sene
To Stapylfforde they took the weye ryht
And as I fynde, he loggyed ther al nyht

At the cheff maner off that litil toun
Weel receyued with besy attendance
And he that hadde the domynacion
Off thilke village lay in gret penance
Thoruh old syknesse but off al greuance
Wher he so longe afforn lay langursshyng
Was maad al hool be myracle off this kyng

And whan he was by grace thus recuryd
Ffull devoutly / in al his beste wise
Made his avough, and hertly hath assuryd
That litil maner hoosly to a mortyse
With the revenuis / as Cawse shyft devyse
To the cherche bzeffly to termyne
Wher the martir / lith hool now in his shryne

Hey glad were whan he was repeyred
To Credysborthe holdyng his weye ryht
ffor long absence, they that were dyspeyres
At his komyng wer maad glad and lyht
Sith ther offryng to hym goth every wyht
Devoutly prayyng, the martir nyht and day
With hem tabyde and never parte away

Baldewynus, a monk off Seynt Denys
Gretly expert in crafft off medycyne
fful provydent off cusayl and ryht wys
Sad off his port, fructuous off doctryne
Affter by grace and influence devyne
Chose off Bury Abbot as I rede
The thrydde in ordre which dide ther succede

To seynt Edward he was pheseuen
To many siknesse he dide remedye
In nyne and twenty wyntur ye may seen
A newe cherche he dyde edefye
Ston brouht fro kand out off Normaudye
By the se and set up on the stronde
At Ratheysdene and caryed forth be londe

By helpe and support off William conquerour
The cherche acomplysshed with his fundacion
Baldewyn dyde his devout labour
Statly to ordeyne for the translacion
Off blyssyd Edmund, yeer from his passion
ffoul tho hundryd twenty and eek fyue
As myn auctour the date doth descryue

Towards the ende, almost off Apryylle
Certeyn prelatis, fro the kyng sent down
This translacion, deuoutly to fullfylle
Off Bedforwthe they entred ben the toun
A thowsand yeer fro the incarnacion
Bynity ouer, by accoutis cleer
With addicion fully, off foue yeer

The feste kept with al the obseruances
By custom vsid, off Antiquyte
I lakke konyng, to telle al circustances
Appertenyng to that solempnyte
The poopis bullys, yaff hem auctoryte
The kyng weel wyllyd, ther was noon obstacle
By cleer report off many fayr myracle

These thynges rekynd, ouhte ynowh suffyse
Vertuously, this mater for to gwide
And to procede in most humble wyse
With dreed and reuence, off ryht as they wer bounde
Out off a chapel that callyd was rotounde
They took the martir, on ther shuldres squar
And to the shryne, deuoutly they it bar

Whych was afforn provyded for the nonys
With clothis off gold, arrayed and pere
And with many ryche precyous stonys
Longyng on to his roial dygnyte
Which off his grace and merciful boute
To our requestis shal thoogh condescende
Geyn al our ennyes this lond for to dyffende

O Gloryous martir which off devout humblesse
Ffor crystes sake were bounde to a tre
With shot off arwes suffredyst gret duresse
Thy blood doun raynyng that routhe it was to se
With purpil colour streyned off cruelte
Was al thy body cristis feith tenhance
O blyssyd kyng off mercyful pite
Pray for thenheritour off Ingelond and ffrance

Settyst a syde al thy royal noblesse
ffor Crystus sake gemme off vyrgynyte
Lefftyst thy kyngdham thy tresour thy rychesse
So feruently brentyst in charyte
That dreed off deth nor duplycyte
Myhte make the trucchh in thy mortal greuance
Wherfore O martir off mercyful bounte
Pray for thenherytour off Inglond and ffrance

Be thow our shield al foreyn ffoon to presse
Our sheeld our pauys castel off suerte
Our portecolys boolewerk off stabylnesse
Gate off dyffence so kepyng the entre
That noon enemy may breke our liberte
O gracyous martir haue alway remembrance
To pray the lord in the celestyal se
ffor thenheryour off Inglond and ffrance

Pray thatt the churche may stonde in parfytnesse
Pray for prynces to kepe ther dygnyte
Vertuously withoute doublynesse
Pray for knyghthod to loue tok ther dextre
Pray for the lawe thatt noon extorsion be
And off marchautis hold iustly the ballance
Pray for the plowh pray for the pouerte
And for thenheryour off Inglond and ffrance

Encresse

Encresse prelatis in ther holynesse
And folk religious in ther humylite
Vertuous wydwes in ther stedfastnesse
Wyues in ther trouthe maydenhod in chastyte
Keep innocentis from al aduersite
Pray for al nedy thow send hem suffisance
By a prerogatyff pray to the Trynyte
ffor thenheritour off Ingelond and ffrance

Pray for Artyffycers in ther besynesse
Trewle to perseuere devoyd off sotylte
ffor labourers teschewen ydylnesse
As they been ordeyned off thos in ther degre
Saue trewe pilgrymes from al aduersite
And maryners from wyndy disturbance
Pray for pes and for tranquyllite
Pray for thenheritour off Inglond and ffrance

Folk at debat reconcyle and redresse
Refourme discordys to pes and vnyte
ffolk languysshyng and bedred for sykenesse
Sende hasty confort to ther infirmyte
ffolk exylyd restore to ther contre
To presonerys mercyful delyuerance
And blyssyd Edmund in long prosperyte
Conserue thenherytour off Inglond and ffrance

Encresse our kynyng in knyghtly hih prowesse
With al his lordys off the spiritalte
Pray thou to graunte conquest and worthynesse
By ryhtful tytle to al the temporalte
And to promote Henry Ioye and felycyte
Off his two reolmys feith loue and obeyssance
Louŋe to perseuere in his victorious se
As iust enheritour off Ingelond and ffrance

L'envoye

O litel book be fereful quaak for drede
For t'appere in so hyh presence
To alle folk that the shal seen or reede
Submytte thy sylff with humble reuerence
To be refourmyd wher men fynde offence
Meekly requeryyng voyde off presumpcion
Wher thow faylest to do correccion

Haue blak and whyt thow hast noon other weede
Off Tullius motles a dyrk apparence
The heuenly botler callyd Gannymede
The to refresshe lyst do no diligence
Off mercurye the aureat influence
The ten lumyne dystyllet skarsly dou
ffor which be soget to al correccion

God graunte that mercy may thy Iourne spede
With gracious support where men fynde offence
Colour is noon thy brydyl for to lede
Off rethoryk to stonde in thy dyffence
Bareyn off languate nakyd off elloquence
At Elycon welle thow drowh but smal foyson
ffor which be soget to al correccion

Polipheme allas took so gret neede
That Arrtus lyst to haue noon aduertence
The to socoure in so gret a neede
The sugre off Omer was ther off be absence
Dul and vnpulisshed off fructuous sentence
Withoute that fauour and supportacion
Off hardy Resceyt do correccion

Calliope lyst nott hyr hawme shede
The tenbellysshe with colours off cadence
Thy auctour ffadred no floures in the mede
Vnder Pernaso to haue ther assystence
Daucter off muses ffaff hym no licence
ffor reproche the hyl off Cytheron
ffor which he sojtet to al correccion

ffinis libri

Rex.

MVSEVM BRITANNICVM

Souereyn lord / plese to your thoosly heed
And to your gracious / royal magnyfycence
To take this tretys / which a then hope and dreed
Presentyd ys to your hyh excellence
And for kyng Edmundis notable reuerence
Beth to his chyrche, dyffence and champion
Be cause yt ys off your ffundacion

Hudlay Caro